My Personal Best

*Life Lessons from an
All-American Journey*

John Wooden

with

Steve Jamison

McGraw·Hill

New York   Chicago   San Francisco   Lisbon   London   Madrid   Mexico City
Milan   New Delhi   San Juan   Seoul   Singapore   Sydney   Toronto

"There is a choice you have to make, in

everything you do. So keep in the mind that

in the end, the choice you make, makes you."

—Anonymous

I pray thee, O God,
that I may
be beautiful within.

SOCRATES

13

Library of Congress Cataloging-in-Publication Data

Wooden, John R.
    My personal best : life lessons from an all-American journey / John Wooden with
    Steve Jamison.
        p.   cm.
    ISBN 0-07-143792-4
    1. Wooden, John R.   2. Basketball coaches—United States—Biography.
   3. Conduct of life.   I. Jamison, Steve.   II. Title.

    GV884.W66   2004
    796.323′092—dc22   2004000790

7 8 9 0   WCT/WCT 3 2 1 0 9 8 7

ISBN 0-07-143792-4

Interior design by Nick Panos

Photo credits can be found on page 208 and should be considered an extension of this
copyright page.

McGraw-Hill books are available at special quantity discounts to use as premiums and
sales promotions, or for use in corporate training programs. For more information, please
write to the Director of Special Sales, Professional Publishing, McGraw-Hill, Two Penn
Plaza, New York, NY 10121-2298. Or contact your local bookstore.

This book is printed on acid-free paper.

For Inch and Miles
From their friends, Coach Wooden and Steve.

"Coach Wooden really cared about us boys on the team. And he made me practice extra free throws."

—Howard "Monk" Fahrubel (1914–2004) Dayton High School Green Devils, class of 1934 and recipient of the Free Throw Shooting Award

CONTENTS

"Failing to prepare is preparing to fail."

PREFACE
Game of a Lifetime

In the opening minutes of play on October 14, 1910—a Friday—John Robert Wooden entered the game. According to the official program, he weighed in at exactly 13 pounds and measured 19½ inches. It has been underway for almost a century now, and John Wooden is having one of the greatest games anyone has ever played.

When it started, a loaf of bread cost a nickel, the Dow Jones average was 81, and you could mail a letter for 2 cents. Milk was free if you owned a cow, and the Wooden family, tenant farmers on the Indiana prairie, did.

As the Dow Jones rose along with the price of bread and everything else, John Wooden grew up and became a singular and towering figure in American sports. In fact, his impact today goes beyond sports to education, business, and life.

Put simply, he's an American icon hailed as "The Greatest Coach of The 20th Century" and awarded the Presidential Medal of Freedom at the White House. *Sports Illustrated's* Rick Reilly is blunt: "There has never been a finer coach in American sports than John Wooden. Nor a finer man."

Coach Wooden's UCLA teams soared to heights that may never be reached again and set records that may stand forever: 10 national championships in twelve years (seven of them occurring in a row); an 88-game winning streak; 38 consecutive wins in NCAA March Madness tournaments; 4 perfect seasons. Overall, a lifetime winning percentage of more than .800 with only one losing season—his very first year.

Before that, Johnny Wooden starred as a three-time All-American at Purdue University (captain of the 1932 national championship team). This followed his selection—twice—as an All-State high school player and member of the Indiana state champion Martinsville basketball team.

And, as the years went on, the great love he shared together with Nell brought the arrival of Nan and Jim and then grandchildren and great-grandchildren. Of course, always there has been his teaching.

This résumé and these accolades attached to one person would seem impossible except, as we know, they're true. Like I said, he's having one of the greatest games anyone has ever played.

So, how did this happen—a "John Wooden"—whose accomplishments almost defy comprehension?

In his poem "The Layers," Stanley Kunitz, twice America's poet laureate, describes a "principle of being" that resides in each of us—who we really are at heart (and in our hearts); our "indestructible essence." In *My Personal Best*, John Wooden reveals his own "principle of being" in a manner so vivid and direct it's almost three-dimensional. In the process, we find out how a "John Wooden" happened.

In preparing the book with Coach, more than five thousand photographs were evaluated; many he had never seen before. The very best of them, those that evoked special insights and memories are presented here along with his reflections on the people who shaped his life and taught him the lessons he learned (and later shared) on this All-American journey.

At core, Coach Wooden's story is primarily about success—how to define, pursue, and achieve it. *My Personal Best* tells how he did, and does it, and how we can too.

The message he brings is radical because beating an opponent, achieving glory, or accumulating power and wealth have never been his ultimate goals. In fact, they are not goals, but by-products of success as he defines it.

John Wooden is no wizard, uses no magic. In fact, the opposite is true: "It starts with hard work and enthusiasm," he cautions us. "There is no trick, no easy way to achieve competitive greatness and success in basketball or life."

No easy way, perhaps, but there is a way—it is the way of Wooden.

—Steve Jamison

ACKNOWLEDGMENTS

Nan Wooden Muehlhausen, Jim Wooden, Mr. and Mrs. Bill Wooden, Dan and Maurice "Cat" Wooden, and Mike Curtis

Mary Jean and Ev Edstrom; Pat, Kris, Kate, Kim Edstrom; and Mike Cronen

Los Angeles
Whitney Lee, The Fielding Agency

Martinsville, Indiana
Elmer Reynolds, Larry Maxwell, Randy Taylor, Don Alkire, Mrs. William E. (Bobbie) Poe, Barb Gray, Jean Lafery, David Ross, Bette Nunn, and Marta Johnson

Mooresville, Indiana
Jack and Fran Abbott (Mr. Earl Warriner's daughter)

Purdue University
Elliot Bloom, Assistant Sports Information Director; Katherine Markee, Special Collections Library, Dayton, Kentucky; Tom Madison, Principal, Dayton High School; and Charlie Tharp

South Bend, Indiana
Jim Powers, Ed Ehlers, and Mrs. Walt (Dort) Kindy

Terre Haute, Indiana, Indiana State University
Susan David, ISU Arches, Athletic Photograph Collection

UCLA

Scott Quintard, photographer, ASUCLA; Todd Cheney, ASUCLA; Dan Guerrero, Director of Athletics; Marc Dellins, Director, Sports Information; Bill Bennett, Associate Sports Information Director; Freddie Sulit, Art Director, UCLA Hall of Fame; and Arvli Ward, Director, Student Media, UCLA

New Castle, Indiana, Indiana Basketball Hall of Fame

Roger Dickenson and Sharon Roberts

Sports Illustrated

Prem Kalliat

AP Worldwide Photo

Bill Fitzgerald

Los Angeles Times

Bill Dwyre and Kate McCarthy

Springfield, Massachusetts, Naismith Memorial Basketball Hall of Fame

Matt Zeysing

Oak View, California

Jimi Giannatti

Naismith Memorial Basketball Hall of Fame

Robin Jonathan Deutsch

INDIANA FARM BOY

LESSONS FROM LONG AGO

I was raised on oatmeal. My brothers—Maurice, Daniel, and Billy—and I had oatmeal for breakfast nearly every morning on our farm back in Centerton, Indiana. I raised my own children on oatmeal. Some things don't change; some lessons remain the same. Those my father taught many years ago may seem old-fashioned now, but like oatmeal, they still work.

Joshua Hugh Wooden was a farmer—honest, hardworking, and fair. I never heard him speak an unkind word about another person, even on those occasions when he had every reason to. Dad came as close to living the Golden Rule as anyone I've ever known. He was strong enough to bend a thick iron bar with his bare hands, but he was also a very gentle man who read poetry to his four sons at night. He loved his family deeply.

My father had a great appreciation for good books, knowledge, and education. Basketball? Enough to knock the bottom out of an old Van

The greatest thing a father can do for his children is to love their mother; Dad did.

Camp tomato basket and nail it to the hayloft in the barn. Baseball was his favorite sport, unless you count checkers as a sport—which he did. At a time when Indiana was completely basketball crazy, Dad built a baseball diamond out behind the barn. Branch McCracken, a future Hall of Fame athlete and coach, and other local boys from around Centerton, Hazelwood, Martinsville, and Monrovia would come by on weekends to play ball and eat watermelon.

But even baseball, in Dad's opinion, was just for play, a diversion. In his house there was a time for chores, a time for study, and then a time for play. Play came only when the first two had been completed.

A HARD GOOD LIFE

Our farm was sixty-five Indiana acres of wheat, corn, alfalfa, timothy, and potatoes. A narrow dirt road cut through the fields and past our white farmhouse with its sparse living room and kitchen—a black pot-belly stove in the former, a wood-burning stove for cooking in the latter. There were two small bedrooms for the six of us; my brothers and I slept two to a bed. Near our old barn was a smokehouse for curing meat, and next to that, a well where we pumped our water by hand. Over to the side, all by itself, was the outhouse—a three-holer.

We had no electricity, plumbing, or conveniences, and for entertainment Dad read books to us in the evening by the light of a coal-oil lamp. Sometimes we'd hear Lord Alfred Tennyson's *Idylls of the King*, Edgar Allan Poe's "The Raven," or even William Shakespeare. Before

we were sent off to bed, he'd always include a verse or two from the Good Book.

On those bitter cold nights when the winter winds whistled across our fields, Dad would heat bricks on the pot-belly stove and wrap them in towels. He'd place the bricks at the foot of our beds, under the thick wool quilts Mother had sewn, to keep us warm.

A TRUE COMPASS

Dad was the best man I ever knew, the one who set the course that guided me through life—what I believe, what I do, and how I do it. In so many ways he made everything happen. And he did it by teaching us in word and deed that the simplest virtues and values were the most important ones.

"Don't try to be better than somebody else, but never cease trying to be the best you can be."

—JOSHUA WOODEN

Joshua Hugh Wooden died long before the University of California–Los Angeles (UCLA) won a men's college basketball championship. Do I wish he'd lived to see me coach a team to a national title? Yes, but it wouldn't have mattered so much to him.

His priorities were different. Material things and public notice meant little. Education was important. Family was important. Outscoring someone in a basketball game, even for a national championship, had much less significance. Dad lived long enough to see me accomplish what was important to him. Nevertheless, he was responsible for the good things that happened to me as a coach. Therefore, it surprises people that I received hardly any basketball instruction from Dad—no tips on jump shots, free throws, or anything else. He seldom attended games and was only slightly interested in results. His concern and guidance were deeper.

In those early days, Dad's message about basketball—and life—was this: "Johnny, don't try to be better than somebody else, but never cease trying to be the best *you* can be. You have control over that. The other

Joshua Hugh Wooden taught character mostly by his own example.

you don't." It was simple advice: work hard, very hard, at those things I can control and don't lose sleep over the rest of it. His advice was easier said than done, but very good advice.

Then he would usually add, as he talked to us at the kitchen table, "Boys, always try to learn from others, because you'll never know a thing that you didn't learn from somebody else—even if it's what *not* to do." I believed him and took his advice to heart and later tried to teach the same message.

At Dayton High School, South Bend Central High School, Indiana State Teachers College, and UCLA, those under my supervision knew I asked for an accountability above outscoring an opponent or getting a better grade than the person across the aisle. "Try your hardest. Make the effort. Do your best," I'd tell them. "The score cannot make you a loser when you do that; it cannot make you a winner if you do less." I still believe this.

Some have suggested that one of the reasons UCLA often outscored opponents was that I never stressed outscoring opponents—that is, "beating" someone else or "needing" to win a game. I don't know if that's true or not. Try your hardest, make the effort, do your best. That's what I stressed, and it came from Dad.

"TRY YOUR HARDEST. MAKE THE EFFORT. DO YOUR BEST."

Today, almost a century after he first taught that lesson to me, I believe his advice is still good as gold. I learned so much from my father, but that may be his strongest lesson. It's hard to say.

A MOTHER'S EXAMPLE

Roxie Anna Wooden, my mother, lost her two young daughters—my sisters—early on. Diphtheria killed Cordelia before her third birthday. My youngest sister died before she even had a name. They were buried in the Centerton cemetery not far from our farm. Today my parents lie next to them.

I doubt if Mother ever really recovered from the deaths of her two little girls. Perhaps she survived because farm life offered no time for self-pity. Maybe she survived because of her strength and her religion.

Like my father, Mother placed her faith in the Good Lord, and they taught us to do the same.

The food we ate we grew. Dad had about thirty hogs, four or five milk cows, lots of chickens, and some mules for field work—no tractor for plowing, no automobile for driving. Mother's garden was next to our farmhouse and was bigger than the house. Peas, carrots, tomatoes, squash, beans, celery, radishes, and strawberries were grown, eaten, or canned and stored down in the fruit cellar. She even canned beef and pork. Chicken was the only fresh meat we ate year-round, and Mother cooked it a hundred different ways. I liked it every way she made it, especially roast chicken. In fact, I still like roast chicken. Occasionally Dad would shoot squirrel, rabbit, or quail, which added a little variety to our kitchen table.

Mother baked our bread and Dad churned our butter. When the bread was hot out of the stove, we'd spread the butter on thick and cover it with homemade strawberry jam, or blackberry or raspberry. I loved the heels of the loaf, still warm and soft with plenty of sweet fresh butter. I still love the heels, even if the bread is from a store. And I miss Mother's persimmon pudding, peach cobblers, and homemade ice cream.

Mom faced the great burden placed on her without complaint.

She sewed most of our clothing. In fact, I don't remember her ever buying a new dress for herself. Only on rare occasion did she purchase new shoes. When she did, they had to last her a long time and so did ours.

Joshua Hugh and Roxie Anna Wooden's lives were hard, but for my brothers and me, growing up on that little farm in Centerton was almost perfect.

LESSONS IN THE LOSS

The end came suddenly. Bad vaccination serum killed the hogs, drought stunted the crops, and the bank took the farm. In those days there was no insurance for this kind of trouble, so we lost everything. Those were very hard times for our family, and the Great Depression hadn't even begun.

Through it all, Dad never winced. He laid no blame on the merchant who had sold him the bad serum, didn't curse the weather, and had no hatred toward the banker. My father had done his best, but things went bad. "Blaming, cursing, hating doesn't help you," he'd say. "It hurts you." His example is deeply imbedded in my mind and, I hope, reflected in my behavior.

Never lie.
Never cheat.
Never steal.

Don't whine.
Don't complain.
Don't make excuses.

He was a living model of his own "two sets of threes"—brief instructions that he felt were basic to decent behavior. My brothers and I heard his two sets of threes often while we were growing up—not as often as we ate oatmeal, but enough that we remembered them: "Never lie. Never cheat. Never steal," was his first set. "Don't whine. Don't complain. Don't make excuses," was the second set. He believed you should do your best, and if the results were unsatisfactory, keep quiet about it and work harder next time.

As instructive as it was to hear him recite the two sets of threes, seeing him abide by them as he lost the farm had a most powerful effect on me. That's where I came to see that what you do is more important than what you say you'll do. People say they'll do all kinds of things.

Centerton's seventh and eighth graders. I'm in the front row, second from the left.

MY FIRST COACH
PRINCIPAL EARL WARRINER

Centerton Grade School—a three-room schoolhouse—was a half mile up the road from our farm. The principal was Mr. Earl Warriner, a disciplinarian who was strict, but fair. When he gave it to you, you had it coming. On those occasions he'd walk outside and cut a switch from the hedge, trim off its thorns with his silver pocketknife, and then let you have it across the backside a few times. It stung even though I always wore heavy denim overalls.

Mr. Warriner was a feisty boxer, excellent athlete, and spirited competitor. He was also well-liked and respected, and a veteran of World War I. At the time, I didn't know what a mentor was, but he became one for me, a positive and guiding influence throughout my life.

Mr. Warriner (right) wasn't afraid to stand up for what he believed.

When I was eleven, my father gave me permission to play on the Centerton basketball team under Mr. Warriner's supervision. The team had eight or nine boys, depending on the day and how the fall harvest was coming along. We played on a dirt court next to the schoolhouse and had to rake off branches, leaves, and sticks before a game. In the late fall, sometimes it would start snowing while we were playing, but we would keep right on going.

Our basketball had a heavy cover of thick brown leather and was about the same size as today's ball—only it wouldn't stay that size. As it gradually lost air, we'd unlace it and use a shoehorn to pry the bladder's air tube out, put it between our lips and blow hard, tie a rubber band around the tube, and knead it back under the cover laces. Unfortunately, it got out-of-round easily, picked up dirt quickly, and became heavier as the game wore on. Later, as an All-American at Purdue University, I received considerable attention for my dribbling skills. Learning with a lopsided basketball on a dirt court with potholes and patches of snow may have been why I became a pretty fair dribbler.

I LEARNED MY FIRST LESSON ABOUT COACHING ON THIS DIRT COURT NEXT TO CENTERTON GRADE SCH

EDUCATION BEFORE SPORTS

As a teacher, coach, principal, and athlete, Mr. Warriner felt that while sports could be worthwhile, true education was obtained only in the classroom. Therefore, he allowed no boy to practice or play without specific permission from teachers. Schoolwork had to be completed and classes attended. Only then would he give you the privilege of walking on his dirt court to play basketball. Later, when I was coaching, my emphasis on academics reflected Mr. Warriner's own priorities (as well as Dad's). There's a reason *student* comes first in the word *student-athlete*: education comes before sports—or at least it should.

There's a reason student *comes first in the word* student-athlete: *education comes before sports.*

Nevertheless, when Mr. Warriner did give me permission to play basketball, I learned more than x's and o's.

MY FIRST LESSON IN COACHING

I was one of the "guns" on our pint-size team, and as the top scorer—five or six points a game—I was getting a big head about it, probably cocky.

One of our grade-school rivals, Hazelwood, was scheduled for a game at Centerton at 2 P.M. That morning, however, their principal called and cancelled because Hazelwood's truck had broken down. As usual, I walked back to our farm at noon for lunch and then returned to school without my basketball jersey—a little homemade bib we wore over our shirts. But things had changed. Mr. Warriner announced the Hazelwood truck was fixed and the game was on.

I didn't feel like running right back home, so I informed him I couldn't play because my jersey was at the farm. I assumed—hoped—Mr. Warriner would let me play without it or send one of the other kids back to get it. As Centerton's top scorer, I was looking for a little special treatment that I felt I deserved.

Mr. Warriner studied me for a moment and then turned to my friend, Freddie Gooch: "Gooch, got your jersey?" Wearing Freddie's jersey was an option I hadn't considered, but one that would save me some effort.

Freddie replied, "Yes, Mr. Warriner, my jersey's out in the coat room."

"Good, you play for Wooden today. He didn't bring his jersey," Mr. Warriner instructed as he looked me in the eye. Of course, he knew exactly what I was trying to pull.

My grade school friends. I'm on the right, wearing a beanie.

Freddie Gooch jumped out of his chair, while I turned and ran out of the classroom and up the road as hard as I could, grabbed my jersey, and ran back even harder. Hazelwood arrived, I took a few shots, put on my "uniform," and was ready to play. When Mr. Warriner announced Centerton's starting lineup, however, my name was missing—I'd been benched. Freddie Gooch was taking my place.

NO PLAYER IS BIGGER OR BETTER THAN THE TEAM.

Coach Warriner let me sit on the bench during the first quarter and second quarter. Freddie didn't score a point. The short halftime came and went. I sat on the bench through the third quarter. Finally, in the fourth quarter with time running out and Centerton behind by two points, I swallowed my pride.

Running up to Mr. Warriner, I pleaded, "If you put me in there, we can still win this game." He didn't look at me as he calmly replied, "Oh yes, Johnny, I know we can, but there are some things more important than winning a game. Besides, you're probably tired from running home for your jersey. Now go sit down and rest." A few minutes later the game was over—Centerton lost.

I didn't realize it, but the lessons of that day stuck with me: no player is bigger or better than the team. And just as important, I came to understand that the bench is a coach's best friend. If there are two more important coaching concepts in the game, I don't know what they are.

And I learned them sitting on the bench next to a dirt court when I was eleven years old.

Coach Warriner had the courage of his convictions. If it meant losing a little grade-school basketball game, fine. But he had courage on big issues too.

THE COURAGE TO QUIT

When he later became principal of Green Township Grade School, one of the boys got into some serious trouble, and Mr. Warriner expelled him. The boy's father was on the township's school board and barged into Mr. Warriner's office with a threat: "I'll have your job if you don't take my son back," he shouted.

Mr. Warriner replied, "What your son did was bad. He's not returning until I say so and as far as my job is concerned, you can have it!" And he resigned.

One year later when the boy's father was off the school board, Mr. Warriner agreed to return as principal. He was very much like my dad when it came to standing up for what he believed in. For me, their examples were important as the years went by. These men whom I admired so much were willing to make the hard choices and suffer consequences for doing the right thing.

GRADUATION GIFTS

When I graduated from Centerton, it was a big occasion because in those days a grade-schooler who lived in the country didn't automatically go to high school, let alone college. Grade school graduation was noted with a little ceremony and celebration.

Seek clarity of thought, fill your heart with love and compassion for others, be honest and fair, and trust in the Good Lord.

Parents usually wanted to give their children a gift of some kind, but there was little money in our house for this sort of thing. Nevertheless, Dad gave me something of lasting significance—advice, or wisdom, that I've tried to live my life by. It came on a crisp, white three-by-five-inch card. On one side he had copied down a poem that he loved by the Reverend Henry Van Dyke:

Four things a man must learn to do
If he would make his life more true:
To think without confusion clearly,
To love his fellow man sincerely,
To act from honest motives purely,
To trust in God and Heaven securely.

Over the years, the poem's message made more and more sense: seek clarity of thought, fill your heart with love and compassion for others, be honest and fair, and trust in the Good Lord. Goodness gracious, what powerful advice this is.

I turned the little white card over and saw that Dad had also written down the creed he so often shared with my brothers and me: seven simple rules to follow in life. As I began to read it, he said, "Johnny, try and live up to these and you'll do all right."

Dad's Seven-Point Creed:

1. Be true to yourself.
2. Help others.
3. Make each day your masterpiece.
4. Drink deeply from good books, especially the Bible.
5. Make friendship a fine art.
6. Build a shelter against a rainy day.
7. Pray for guidance, and count and give thanks for your blessings every day.

I didn't fully understand how profound Dad's seven-point creed was for many years, until I was an adult raising a family, teaching, and coaching. As it slowly became a part of me, however, that part of me improved.

At the end of the little grade-school ceremony, after we had celebrated with cookies and lemonade and were getting ready to walk back to our farm, Dad handed me another gift: a two-dollar bill with a lot of wear on it. Cash was scarce and two dollars was a lot of money. It was a great graduation day. The two-dollar bill is still in the family, and Dad's seven-point creed is still in my heart. Today when people ask if I was able to live up to his advice, I quote this poem:

I'm not what I ought to be,
Not what I want to be,
Not what I'm going to be,
But I am thankful that I'm better than I used to be.

When the little graduation party at Centerton Grade School was over, we walked back down the road to our farm, changed clothes, and got back to the chores.

Centerton School where I
... taught for seven years

CENTERTON SCHOOL

MARTINSVILLE
CITY OF
MINERAL WATER

3

HIGH SCHOOL HERO

COACH GLENN CURTIS

A traveling carnival came to nearby Martinsville every year on the Fourth of July with fireworks, a giant Ferris wheel, and sideshow attractions. One of the most popular attractions was inside a little tent, where for a nickel you could see a man pull a long, black snake out of a tin bucket full of snakes.

As the crowd hushed, he slowly brought it closer and closer to his face until the snake was just inches from his lips. Then, with the snake writhing and flicking its tongue, the man would suddenly bite off its head. The crowd would gasp as he spit the head into another bucket and began walking among the spectators, swinging the snake back and forth. People would start screaming and yelling and hollering; some even fainted right out of their chairs. But the emotion and excitement in that tent was nothing compared to what happened during high school basketball games when I was a teenager.

This will be hard to believe, but in the 1920s the Indiana State High School Championship—and the games leading up to it—was as wild as any National Collegiate Athletic Association (NCAA) March Madness Final Four I've ever been involved with, and I've been in twelve of them. It was as if a fever hit our whole state at once.

Hoosiers were nutty about basketball. "Ripley's Believe It or Not" claimed that in Martinsville, Indiana, our newly constructed red brick basketball gym on South Main Street could hold 5,520 spectators, which was 300 more people than lived in the town itself. Fans who jammed into the new gymnasium could almost reach out and touch players racing by during a game. The court was polished hardwood, modern bright lights hung from the ceiling, and the ball was perfectly round. This was quite a change from Mr. Warriner's little dirt court in Centerton—and it's where I played basketball as a member of the Martinsville Artesians.

In 1926, 1927, and 1928, Martinsville High School battled all the way into the finals of the Indiana state basketball tournament. Our coach was Glenn Curtis, whose nickname was the Ol' Fox.

Coach Glenn Curtis.

LIVING IN MARTINSVILLE

We had moved into Martinsville my sophomore year, after Dad lost the farm and found work at the Home Lawn Sanitarium, one of the local health spas whose artesian waters and treatments drew visitors from Chicago, New York, and even Europe. Martinsville was known for not only its mineral waters but also its goldfish and, because of the goldfish, its frog legs.

Raising goldfish for sale was a big business in Martinsville. In fact, the *Queen Mary* supposedly had our goldfish on board as an attraction during its maiden voyage. Grassyfork Fisheries was the world's largest goldfish producer, which required big ponds that in turn attracted frogs who lived on the edge of the water. Local cooks would find well-fed frogs and gig 'em—spear the frog—and cook the legs. Fixed right, they're almost as good as roast chicken.

But nothing topped high school basketball in Martinsville, not mineral springs, health spas, goldfish, or frog legs. Basketball was king everywhere—except in the home of Joshua Hugh Wooden. Education remained first for Dad, and he never let Maurice, Daniel, Billy, or me forget that. However, that didn't mean basketball was off my mind. I was sixteen years old, and a member of one of the best high school teams in Indiana.

HIGH SCHOOL BASKETBALL

Glenn Curtis was among the top coaches in the state. Very few had won a single Indiana state high school championship, but he already had two when I joined the Artesians in 1926. My nickname was "Pert," as in "impertinent."

During my sophomore year I got into a fight during practice with one of the starters, a big guy who occasionally used dirty tactics. We went at it hard until Coach Curtis came over, broke up the fight, and told me to apologize for starting it. I felt the other player was in the wrong—tripping me intentionally—and refused to say I was sorry, even though he claimed it was an accident. I didn't believe it. Finally, I got so worked up that I ripped off my jersey; took off my shoes, socks, and trunks; and threw them down in front of Coach Curtis. Then I stalked off the court. How he kept from laughing as I headed to the locker room nearly naked, I don't know.

Fortunately, Glenn Curtis understood human nature pretty well. After letting me think about it a few days, he saw me in the hallway and said, "Johnny, let's forget about what happened the other day and get back to

Nell put my picture in her high school diary.

practice this afternoon." Of course, I was more than eager to forget about it. Like all good coaches, he understood people very well.

GETTING DOWN TO BASICS

Coach Curtis broke basketball down into its basic elements and then practiced and perfected each one. After a while he'd put the pieces back together into a whole. This was uncommon in those early days of the game. Before he would let five players work together as a team, we had to perfect every basic skill he could think of—passing, defending, rebounding, making all the different types of shots, and more.

Coach Curtis stressed what to do when you aren't shooting and don't have the ball. In fact, his Artesians may have spent more time practicing without the basketball than with it. Maybe that's why they called him the Ol' Fox, but I don't like that nickname, because it implies trickery or guile. There's nothing tricky about teaching the basics. It requires only hard work and repetition. He was a teacher, not a "fox."

POETRY IN MOTION

Glenn Curtis also had a knack for motivating players with poetry and could find a verse or phrase, even an entire poem, by Grantland Rice that he would read before a game or at halftime. Although my father introduced poetry to my brothers and me, Coach Curtis was the first person I knew who used it to win basketball games. His poetry always got the players to put out more than we knew we had in us. One of my favorites ended with this verse:

> For when the one Great Scorer
> Comes to write against your name,
> He writes not that you won or lost,
> But how you played the game.

That poem sums up how I feel about competition in sports or anything else.

FIRST TASTE OF TOURNAMENTS

In 1926 I was a guard on the Martinsville team that reached the finals of the Indiana state basketball tournament. It was held inside the Indianapolis Exposition Center, which was nicknamed the "Cow Barn," because cattle were the usual feature attraction.

The tournament was a free-for-all with no divisions or classifications of high schools—all could participate and most did. Of 777 eligible schools, 719 teams signed up to play in the 1926 state tournament. It was my first experience with competition at that level and intensity. If your team advanced to the final weekend, you would play four games in two days: a game on Friday night, another Saturday morning, another Saturday afternoon, and if you kept winning, you played for the championship on Saturday night in front of more than 15,000 fans—four games in two days, three in one day.

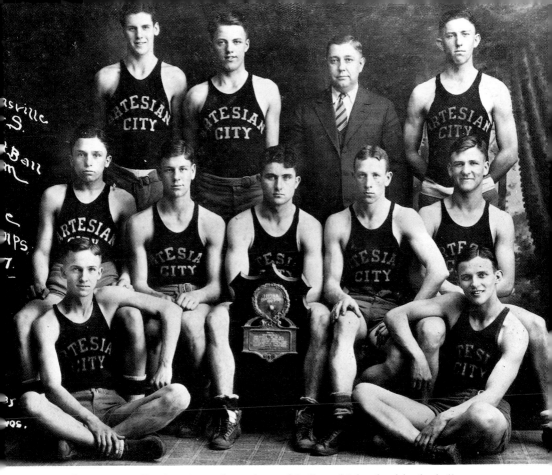

The Martinsville Artesians, champions of Indiana high school basketball,
1927. I'm in the middle row, second from the right.

Most of the 1926 tournament was a blur, but one thing I remember—we lost in the finals to the Marion Giants by seven points, 30–23,
defeated in large part by Charles "Stretch" Murphy, a six-foot-eight
center who seemed as tall as a water tower. (Incidentally, if you're curi-
ous about the low scores, they resulted from the rule in those days that
required a jump ball after each basket.)

PART FOUR   THE INDIANAPOLIS SUNDAY STAR   SPORTS F HOME B NEV

VOL. 21, NO. 236.   SUNDAY MORNING, MARCH 24, 1927.   PRICE—TEN CENTS.

MARTINSVILLE CAPTURES TITLE TILT FROM MUN

The next year, 1927, Martinsville returned to the championship game and outscored Muncie Central, 26–23. The results were headline news on Sunday, March 30, in the state's biggest newspaper, the *Indianapolis Star*.

The Artesians made it to the finals for a third straight time my senior year, 1928, and were favored to repeat as champions. Additionally, my teammates had voted to make me captain, an honor I took seriously.

For the first time, the tournament finals were played at the brand-new Butler University Field House—a gleaming, modern basketball showcase. Again we faced the team we had beaten in 1927, Muncie Central. What happened the second time around, however, was the most disappointing thing I ever experienced as an athlete.

SOMETHING IMPOSSIBLE

In the final seconds of the 1928 Indiana state high school championship, with Martinsville leading by one point, Muncie Central's Charlie Secrist flung a desperation underhand shot from half-court that literally went up to the rafters and came down straight through the hoop. It was impossible.

Here's how impossible it was: in my forty years of coaching basketball at Dayton High School, South Bend Central, Indiana State Teachers College, and UCLA, I never saw anyone make that shot again in competition. But I did see it *once*—Saturday night, March 17, 1928, in the final seconds of the Indiana state high school championship. Martinsville lost 13–12. Muncie Central fans were nearly hysterical at the buzzer.

The loss in the finals of the 1928 Indiana championship game was the most painful thing that ever happened to me as an athlete.

In our locker room afterward, the Artesians, stunned and almost grieving, sat on the benches holding towels over their faces as they wept. Charlie Secrist's last-second shot had been crushing, and all of the players just quietly lowered their heads and cried. All but one.

I couldn't cry. The loss hurt me deeply inside, but I also knew I'd done the best I could do. Disappointed? Yes. Devastated or depressed? No. Dad taught us on the farm, "Don't worry about being better than somebody else, but never cease trying to be the best *you* can be." I had done that. Now as a member of the Martinsville Artesians basketball team, Dad's instructions and example were put to the test.

You lose, you feel bad—sometimes very, very bad. But a much worse feeling is knowing that you haven't done everything you possibly could have done to prepare and compete.

I had done what my father taught me to do, including his two sets of threes, one of which was don't whine, don't complain, don't make excuses. That loss in the 1928 Indiana state high school championships, when the Artesians were defending champions and I was their captain, is still painful to recall. But I couldn't cry. Dad didn't cry when he lost the farm. How could I now?

You lose, you feel bad—sometimes very, very bad. But a much worse feeling is knowing you haven't done everything you possibly could have done to prepare and compete.

4

TRUE LOVE

Nellie Riley was my high school sweetheart and the only girl I ever loved or wanted to love. Some kind of strong spark happened the first time we met. That spark never left—it's still in me. Whatever basketball gave, and it gave plenty, Nellie Riley gave me more and meant more; but that spark almost didn't happen.

I had seen her at Martinsville High School when I was a freshman and still on the farm. I thought, "Whoa, that's a cute girl." At the summer carnival I saw her again, but I didn't think she'd give sour apples for me, a farm boy who was extremely shy.

It turned out she'd also noticed me and was interested enough to do something about it. Nellie wasn't shy. She convinced her very best friend, Mary Schnaiter, to have her older brother, Jack, drive the three of them out to our farm in Centerton on a scorching July afternoon. When they arrived, I was out in the cornfield, hooked up behind either Jack or Kate, our mules. It was hot and muggy, and I'd been plowing up and down all day—my boots and overalls were covered with dirt, and I was dripping sweat. The three of them waved for me to come over by the car, but I acted as if they weren't there and slowly started plowing up a corn row in the opposite direction. After a while, they drove away.

That fall when school started, Nellie stopped me in the hallway as I was heading into Mr. Scheidler's history class and asked why I had been so rude—why I hadn't come over to their car to say hello. I hemmed and hawed a little bit, but then told the truth, "I was all dirty and sweaty," I said. "I thought you'd probably make fun of me."

Nell had a very sweet look on her face and said softy, "Johnny, I would never make fun of you. Never."

Something happened in me right then—that spark that has never gone away. We began walking to and from high school together and occasionally downtown to the Grace Theatre for a Tom Mix or Charlie Chaplin movie. When I didn't have twenty cents for tickets, I'd run ahead to the box office and ask the ticket taker, "Could I pay you later?" In those days you could do that. Sometimes we'd go to Wick's Candy Kitchen or Shireman's Ice Cream Parlor where they popped popcorn outside on Saturdays to attract customers. But mostly we'd just sit on the swing of the Rileys' porch, holding hands and talking.

We began going steady in a sense—in the sense that I was going steady with Nell but she wasn't going steady with me. I really didn't like it, but I understood because Nell was very popular and I was grounded during the long basketball season. Not only did Coach Curtis impose an 8 P.M. curfew, but he also prohibited Artesian players from going out on dates during the entire season.

Of course, everyone on the team broke the second rule, but it was tougher for Nellie and me because Coach Curtis lived a few yards from the Riley house. He could see right into their kitchen from his dining room window.

During the entire basketball season, Nellie and I made very sure we stayed out of the Rileys' kitchen.

Nell joined the high school pep band to get a courtside seat for the Artesians' games, so she could be up close to watch me play. Her musical skills were questionable enough that friends described her as an "alleged" cornetist, who only held the instrument to her lips and pretended to play. It didn't matter—she had a front row seat for all my games.

She was a good ukulele player, however, and a member of the Girls Ukulele Band. Unfortunately, playing the uke didn't get her a front row seat, and it was during those games we started a little ritual that became

a part of our lives. Just before each game, Coach Curtis gathered our team in a huddle for last-second instructions and perhaps a poem. I began positioning myself in the huddle so I could see Nellie in the band's cornet section. When we made eye contact she'd give me a little thumbs-up, and I'd wink or nod back at her. That carried right through to the last game I ever coached.

It became clear to everyone at Martinsville High School that Nell and I were meant for each other. In fact, I never even got around to proposing marriage. We simply agreed during my senior year that when I finished college we'd see the preacher. Nell and I were together through everything that followed—high school, college, family, friends, and my life teaching and coaching.

She is the greatest thing that ever happened to me.

No written word nor spoken plea

    Can teach our youth what they should be.

Nor all the books on all the shelves

    It's what the teachers are themselves.

5

INTEGRITY, TEAM SPIRIT,
AND PIGGY LAMBERT

When asked, I tell people, "I'm a Hoosier at heart, but the Bruins are in my blood." However, the Boilermakers of Purdue University are right there next to both of them.

I wanted to become a civil engineer, and Purdue had an exceptional school of engineering. The Boilermakers also had an exceptional coach teaching an exciting way of playing basketball—the fast break—and wanted to play it. Ward "Piggy" Lambert became the third of the dear coaches and mentors whose impact on me was so profound. He was as principled a coach as any I've ever known.

TRUE TO HIS BELIEFS

For example, when tournaments were being held at New York's Madison Square Garden and his Big Ten champion Purdue Boilermakers were invited, he refused to participate. He felt Madison Square Garden's commercialization invited temptation and trouble for college athletes—first and foremost, gambling. His was not an easy decision to make—alumni loved the publicity, players wanted to visit New York City, and administrators liked the money that tournament appearances produced.

I doubt if Coach Lambert could have found one other person on the Purdue campus in West Lafayette who supported him. It didn't matter.

Ward Lambert, a coach whose teams won or shared eleven Big Ten championships and who was later inducted into the Hall of Fame, refused to take his Boilermakers to New York's Madison Square Garden. He simply believed that it was the wrong kind of environment for his young players.

Later, scandal hit several of the teams involved with the tournament and many of their athletes were hurt. Coach Lambert's instincts had been correct. More important, he had the strength to stick to his guns when he was all alone. I saw him demonstrate this quality many times.

Our freshman basketball squad. I'm in the front row, fifth from the right.

TEAM SPIRIT

Coach Lambert's great concern for the welfare of his players was coupled with his constant emphasis on team unity and togetherness, equality and sacrifice. He taught that every man on the squad counts, each can make a contribution, and no one is superior to another (this applied, of course, to a top-scoring guard whose name was Johnny Wooden). The result was a dedication and commitment to the team by its members—every one of us—that was fierce and powerful.

Make no mistake, Piggy Lambert was extremely competitive—he wanted to win basketball games. But he had an even greater commitment to the well-being of his players beyond basketball to the classroom, and beyond the classroom to our future. And we knew it. Piggy Lambert loved us.

My respect for Coach Lambert has grown even stronger over the years as I've come to recognize his authentic ability to transform individuals in a positive way, both for their own good and for that of the team. He genuinely cared about those under his supervision. For me, he is the model of what a great coach and teacher can be.

FROM ENGINEERING TO ENGLISH

My hopes for a civil engineering major at Purdue were derailed because part of the requirement included attending engineering camp each summer. June, July, and August were moneymaking months for me—and money was hard to come by in the Depression.

In high school I had washed dishes at the Elks club, packed tomatoes at the Van Camp canning plant, worked the pea pack, laid gravel, and dug sewers. At Purdue, I got hired on as a crew member of the Indiana highway department each summer.

I switched to an English major, which allowed me to pursue a love of reading that included Henry Wadsworth Longfellow, Walt Whitman, Lord Byron, Sir Walter Scott, and, of course, William Shakespeare—an entire semester on *Hamlet*, another on *Macbeth*. All of this was under the supervision of an eccentric scholar at Purdue by the name of Professor Liddell, an international authority on Shakespeare and Chaucer.

Although Professor Liddell was born in Pennsylvania, he attended Oxford University. While there, he adopted many British affectations, which he continued at Purdue. Professor Liddell wore a bowler hat and high-buttoned shoes, and carried a tightly rolled black umbrella even in the middle of winter. He drank tea and cherished the classics, but he also loved baseball because it reminded him of cricket and his beloved England.

Each semester on the first day of class, Professor Liddell would stand behind his podium and announce sternly with a trace of a British accent, "If you pay attention and listen day by day, you'll receive an A or a B. However, if at any time during this semester any one of you disturbs my trend of thought, I won't *ask* you to leave, I'll throw you out the door and you won't get back in. Are there any questions?"

And he meant it—if you were expelled, you did not get back into his classroom. On the other hand, if you made it through the year without interrupting his "trend of thought," you'd do fine because he was a great teacher of the classics.

CONDITIONING

Coach Lambert, like Professor Liddell, also had demands, a much longer and exhausting list that included running us ruthlessly and relentlessly in the gym. He seldom paused to give instructions to the group, but instead pulled individual players out for specific instructions while the others continued pounding up and down the court. Most drills were designed with the dual purpose of perfecting a skill while increasing our conditioning. In fact, the only time he addressed the whole team was just before a game, because he wanted near-constant physical activity during every practice.

Nevertheless, even though his drills were punishing, no player would ever voluntarily take a short breather. If you did, Piggy Lambert would give you a long breather: sitting on the bench watching whoever had taken your place. It was his way of encouraging toughness and conditioning. Knowing this was important to him, I not only worked myself extremely hard in practice, but also avoided alcohol and tobacco and tried to behave off the court.

Before you can be a good leader, you must be a good follower.

I recognized that at five foot ten I was not as tall as many others. "Stretch" Murphy, the player who was such a big part of Marion High School's victory over Martinsville in the 1926 state championship and was now the Purdue center, was almost a foot taller than me. There was nothing I could do about height.

Conditioning was another matter. Although it wouldn't make me taller, conditioning gave me a distinct advantage as the game wore on;

specifically, my opponents wore out. Being fit meant more than being tall when a game was on the line in the final minutes. Eventually this became a trademark of the UCLA Bruins.

During my senior year, Coach Lambert told a faculty meeting he'd never seen a better-conditioned athlete for basketball than John Wooden. It is one of the finest compliments I've ever received.

FUNDAMENTALS

Coach Lambert was a brilliant creator of competitive drills such as simultaneous shooting and rebounding practice. Most players love shooting and hate the physical pounding of rebounding. But Coach Lambert wouldn't let you have the fun of shooting until you fought hard and occasionally bloodied elbows and noses under the basket fighting for rebounds—a great way to motivate players to hone what they hate. Only then would he move you out to shoot with the shooters.

There was no frivolity in his method. I wouldn't say he was stern, but Ward Lambert was very serious all the way through. He was also a constant chatterer who moved up and down the sidelines barking out instructions and advice on precisely what to do and exactly when to do it. His focus on the details of execution—fundamentals—was as relentless as his conditioning drills.

The results were good. Coach Lambert's exciting fast-break style produced a perfect record in the Big Ten during my sophomore year, 1930, and Purdue was considered by many to be the national champion.

Stretch Murphy was the star of that Boilermakers team and my best friend both on and off the court. He also helped me pay for some of my college education by bequeathing his "Walk to Chicago" to me.

PAYING MY WAY

Each year the Purdue football team played the University of Chicago coached by legendary Amos Alonzo Stagg. It was a fierce rivalry that attracted so many Boilermaker fans that the Monon Railroad ran a special train out of Lafayette to Chicago for the big game at Soldier Field.

Stretch had the unofficial rights to sell concessions on the trip, and he passed them down to me when he graduated. That's when I started telling friends that once a year I "walked" to Chicago and back. Of course, I was doing the walking on board the Monon Hoosier Express to Chicago—going up and down the aisles hawking sandwiches, soft drinks, and cigarettes to excited and often inebriated alumni. Prohibition was the law, so I'd wait until they'd had a little bathtub gin and then make my rounds.

One of my biggest moneymakers was something I manufactured myself. I'd go to local department stores that donated gold and black ribbons. They'd throw in a big box of safety pins, and I'd spend several hours cutting and crossing the ribbons to create little lapel pennants in the Purdue colors. They cost me nothing, and I sold them for ten cents each. And I sold plenty.

During the basketball season, I also published and sold the official Purdue program—wrote the copy, sold the ads, and mimeographed it myself. Since I was on the court during games, I enlisted high school kids to sell the programs for a dime apiece. Afterward we'd get together and split up the profits.

During the football season, I made money as a "taper" who wrapped ankles, arms, and legs and then on weekends, I helped paint the football stadium for thirty-five cents an hour. All of this allowed me to pay my way at Purdue.

Nevertheless, it was a struggle and I'm not sure I could have made it without Nell's support and encouragement. While I was at Purdue, she was waiting for me back in Martinsville, sending cards and letters about our future together. I knew that future would be a lot better if I got my degree.

INDIA RUBBER MAN

The Boilermakers were national champions in my sophomore and senior years and twice won the Big Ten Conference championship. My

nickname was the "India Rubber Man" because I seemed to bounce up off the floor immediately after being knocked down. And I got knocked down a lot. Coach Lambert, fearful that I'd get hurt driving hard to the basket and then into the stands, would often put members of the Purdue football team at the end of the court to catch me before my momentum carried me into harm's way.

In spite of the bumps and bruises, cuts and scratches, his fast-break style suited me perfectly. In my senior year, I led the Big Ten in scoring with 154 points. That doesn't seem like much today, but back then it was a lot of baskets. Ward Lambert was changing the game—in those days the kind of speed he was putting on the basketball court was almost radical. Later when I took it to UCLA, it was responsible, in part, for some immediate and surprising success.

THE RIGHT PRIORITIES

Ward Lambert's priorities in basketball were simple: conditioning, fundamentals, and team spirit. His priority as a person was more direct and demanding: stand up for what you believe—even when you stand alone. My college coach was a great builder of teams and men. Ward Lambert knew there was a direct relationship between what it takes to be good basketball player and the requirements for being a good person.

Stand up for what you believe—even when you stand alone.

When I started coaching and teaching, I tried to make his priorities my priorities. Coach Lambert's picture hangs on the wall in my den right next to the photographs of the ten national championship teams I coached at UCLA. He belongs up there.

THE BEST HONOR OF ALL

In 1932 when I graduated from Purdue, I was nineteenth in my class and was awarded the Big Ten medal for scholarship and athletic prowess. The university president, Edward Elliot, personally presented the medal to me.

As a basketball player at Purdue I'd been voted All-American three years in a row and won the scoring title my senior year when Purdue

My Boilermaker buddies. I'm standing second from the left.

was the national champion. I'd also been elected captain of the team in both my junior and senior years. The Big Ten scholarship award, however, meant more to me, because in many ways it honored my father, Joshua Hugh Wooden.

When I was a youngster, Dad's guidance always emphasized the value of books, knowledge, and education. The Big Ten scholarship and athletic prowess medal belonged to him, for those many cold winter nights when he lit the coal-oil lamp and read books to his four sons next to a glowing potbelly stove.

Young people need good models, not critics.

6

A NEW JOB FOR A TERRIBLE COACH

Nellie and I got married on August 8, 1932, at a little church in Indianapolis where Nell's older sister had gotten married—Nell wanted the same preacher. I was twenty-one, Nell was twenty, and we were head over heels in love. In fact, I may not have been able to see straight.

Many years later, someone pointed out that on our marriage certificate under "Occupation," I tried to write "basketball coach" but misspelled the word *basketball*. This from an English major, honor student, and All-American basketball player.

That was of no consequence compared to the financial catastrophe that had struck two days earlier. The Martinsville Trust Company—where I had put my entire life's savings, exactly $909.05—

went bust. When the bank went broke, so did I. At 6 P.M. on August 6, 1932—two days before Nell and I were supposed to get married—I had exactly two dollars to my name, the same two-dollar bill Dad had given me as a graduation gift at Centerton Grade School. I remembered him telling me, "Johnny, as long as you have this you'll never be broke." Technically he was right, but on that particular night I felt broke.

A local businessman took pity on us and helped out. Mary Schnaiter's father, Cliff, invited me to his office for a chat—I had no idea what he had in mind. As we were talking, Mr. Schnaiter slid an envelope across his desk and said, "Johnny, this will get you and Nell started. Pay me back when you're able. No rush."

The two hundred dollars inside the envelope allowed Nell and me to begin our new life together. We were married the next day and even spent a small sum celebrating in Indianapolis listening to the Mills Brothers at the Circle Theatre. Many years later, I kidded them about their performance on my wedding night: "I thought you guys would never get done singing."

The next morning, Nell and I got up early, walked a half mile to the bus station and caught a 6 A.M. ride back to Martinsville. Coach Lambert met us at the station, dropped Nell off at her parents', and drove me to Vincennes, Indiana, for a basketball clinic where I was paid twenty-five dollars to be his demonstrator for a week. So for the first seven days of our married life, Nellie stayed at her parents' home while I bunked at Coach Lambert's basketball camp ninety-two miles away. It seemed a lot farther than ninety two miles and longer than seven days.

Only afterward, did Nell and I head to my new job at Kentucky's Dayton High School where I was an English teacher, athletic director, and coach of baseball, football, track, and basketball. My starting salary was $1,500—$1,200 for teaching English, $300 for coaching. I may have been overpaid for my coaching abilities.

A TERRIBLE MISTAKE

The Green Devils football team had a big lumbering lineman who bullied other classmates and even teammates; he was the kind of player who did only as much as he wanted to do and no more. On a sweltering Kentucky afternoon during the first week of football practice, this young man decided he'd had enough of my whistle blowing, directions, and drills. When I told him to get back to work, he challenged me. He stuck his chin right in my face and snarled, "You're not man enough to make me do it." The whole team was watching us.

I responded emotionally and without thinking, and I am very ashamed of what happened next—a brief but physical altercation. It was terrible behavior from someone trying hard to follow the examples of my coaching mentors. Even more, it went against my father's teaching.

One of his favorite quotes was from Abraham Lincoln: "There is nothing stronger than gentleness." Now, as a brand-new coach—two weeks into the job—I had quickly lost my temper and stooped to violence. It troubled me very deeply.

"There is nothing stronger than gentleness."

—ABRAHAM LINCOLN

These days I'd be fired, rightfully, but on that hot humid afternoon we just moved on and continued practice.

I quickly came to understand I wasn't a good football coach (the stubborn lineman, however, was not the reason) and asked my predecessor, Willard Bass, to come back. As the weeks went along, I heard through the grapevine that whenever one of the Green Devil players gave him any trouble, Coach Bass would warn sternly, "Please don't make me tell Johnny Wooden about this." He was kidding, of course, but I didn't think it was very funny.

A GOOD PLAYER, A BAD COACH

Coaching basketball presented its own challenges, many of which I wasn't prepared for. I not only saw my temper flare up, but I was too critical, impatient, eager to fill players full of information, and quickly irritated when they couldn't absorb it. Since everything had come easily for me as a player, I didn't understand why these young men couldn't do the same. It was extremely upsetting to demonstrate something correctly only to watch them do it incorrectly—over and over. Patience is a most valuable asset for a leader. I lacked it, just as young coaches and teachers usually do.

I was not a yeller or screamer, but I'd complain to others at school about how disappointed I was in the Green Devils. Of course, this got right back to the boys, who in turn became even more dispirited. I had yet to learn that the greatest motivator is a well-deserved pat on the back from someone you respect. Instead, I was quick to criticize, slow to commend.

PATIENCE IS A MOST VALUABLE ASSET FOR A LEADER.

Our results were predictable. As a player at Centerton, Martinsville, and Purdue I'd never been on a team with a losing season. In fact, usually we were fighting for a state or national championship. The Dayton High School Green Devils introduced me to coaching with a losing season. To my credit, I was smart enough to admit the biggest reason we weren't any good was me—I was just a terrible coach.

The high school yearbook reported our results: "Dayton's Greendevil (sic) basketball team went through a discouraging season in 1933. They completed their schedule with only six victories, but suffered eleven defeats. Dayton will attempt to make a better showing next year under the able direction of their coach, John Wooden." At least, they were hoping I could offer "able direction," having seen little of it during my first attempt at coaching.

To add insult to injury, the Green Devils had traveled to Martinsville for a game against the Artesians. In front of a packed crowd—maybe the biggest crowd ever to see a game in the gym where I had been an All-State basketball player—the Green Devils lost 27–17. Their coach was Glenn Curtis—the Ol' Fox. Martinsville went on to win the Indiana state championship that year, but losing in front of my hometown friends and former teammates made the ride back to Dayton seem very long.

THE CLASSROOM COACH

Fortunately, I was better at teaching English. In fact, my coaching skills improved greatly because of what I did in the classroom. Teaching a solid subject such as English forced me to create a detailed schedule and lesson plan and to get things done efficiently without wasting time. I couldn't just amble into class each day without precise preparation.

For example, I had fourteen days to cover *Hamlet*. In college Professor Liddell spent an entire semester teaching that one play. For my Dayton students to have any chance of learning something about Shakespeare, I needed to carefully hone my plan—each hour, nearly each minute. I budgeted my time in the classroom precisely—carefully planning how to cover *Silas Marner*, *A Tale of Two Cities*, poetry, and Shakespeare.

I learned to accommodate the abilities of a wide range of students. My patience grew, my tolerance for boys and girls who had difficulty keeping up with my lesson plan increased, and my understanding of various personalities and how to deal with them expanded. All of this I tried to apply in coaching. I believe that in that first year at Dayton High School I learned more about how to work with people and about myself—my temper, stubbornness, impatience, and desire for immediate results—than any of the thirty-nine years of coaching that followed.

The second season reflected this and produced my very first winning record as a coach: 15–3. The *Dayton Pilot*, our yearbook, proclaimed that "Johnny Wooden, our versatile coach, whipped into shape one of the best teams Dayton has sponsored in recent years." My coaching was hailed as "tip-top" and the Green Devils proclaimed to have "soared to

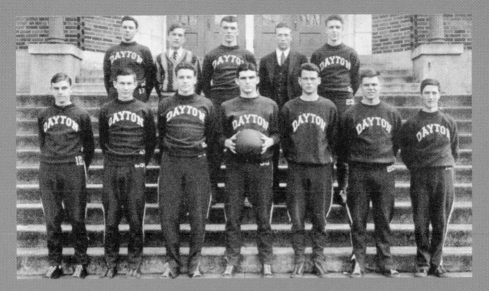

Basketball Story

Dayton's triumphant basketball team soared to great heights in their 1933-34 basketball campaign. They captured fifteen out of eighteen games played.

Having only two regulars left from last season's squad, Johnny Wooden, our versatile coach, whipped into shape one of the best teams Dayton has sponsored in recent years. The team's coolness and efficiency was due in part to Captain Bill Smith, an able leader at all times. Hard fought games, continuous practice, and tip-top coaching placed the team up in the front ranks of local basketball.

Bellevue upset Dayton's first string of victories by a 15 to 11 score. A few games later, Purcell, Cincinnati champs, left Dayton the little end of a 25 to 20 tally. Later in the season, Dayton avenged Bellevue's defeat by demoralizing the Tigers in the return tussle.

In tournament play, because of the strenuousness of the past season, Dayton lagged to some extent, and the bigness of the floor and the sharpshooting of the Bellevue boys was too much. As a result, the Green Devils were put out of the running in the first round.

The Regional Tournament was held at Dayton and the members of our team played host to the visiting teams and helped to make their sojourn here very enjoyable.

Nine men were presented with the "D" for varsity service. They are: Captain Smith, B. Davis, D. Davis, Bertrand, Carmichael, Fahrubel, Stull, Wilson, and Gray.

Four minor letters were awarded to: Beinker, Wolf, Bridewell, and Daughtee.

Following are the records of the first and second teams:

First Team—Won 15 games, lost 3. 481 points scored for an average of 26.7 points per game.

Second Team—Won 14 games, lost 2. 465 points scored for an average of 29 per game.

Howard Fahrubel received a small gold basketball from Mr. Wooden for foul shooting in the games. Bill Smith received one for foul shooting in practice.

great heights" during this "triumphant" year. I had gone from a goat to a hero in a few short months. I had been the hero before, but never the goat.

I had great expectations for the coming season, my third at Dayton, but Indiana came calling—South Bend Central High School offered a teaching and coaching position with a large pay raise that included $2,400 a year as English teacher, athletic director, school comptroller, and baseball and basketball coach. Eventually I even taught tennis.

Nell and I accepted the offer and headed home—but not alone. We were brand-new parents—a threesome with the arrival of our beautiful little daughter, Nancy Ann Wooden.

7

BACK HOME IN (SOUTH BEND) INDIANA

At Dayton High School, I had fallen in love with teaching and coaching. There were great frustrations, setbacks, and embarrassing moments, but the pleasure of teaching young people was more than money could buy. It was joy, pure and simple. In fact, during my entire career as a teacher and coach there were always offers for outside jobs that paid a lot—a lot more money than teaching did. Nell, bless her heart, never once suggested I should change professions.

This was important because had she asked, I would have quit and taken the higher-paying job. Nell seemed to understand that I was meant to be a teacher—she may have known it even more than I did. And this was important because I faced an immediate challenge with my new job.

A CHALLENGING SITUATION

At South Bend Central there was no gymnasium available at the school. Instead we used the stark facilities at a local YMCA, whose unheated locker room was in the dimly lit basement. Hot water was in short supply. During the frigid winter months, players could occasionally see their breath as they changed clothes. Never before or since have I witnessed a team shower and get dressed as fast as those boys did on a subzero morning.

Practice for the Bears began in the early darkness at 6:30 A.M. because the Y's gym was unavailable later. Upstairs we worked practice around hindrances, including a boxing ring, wrestling mats, and gymnastics equipment as well as YMCA members who came in for some exercise.

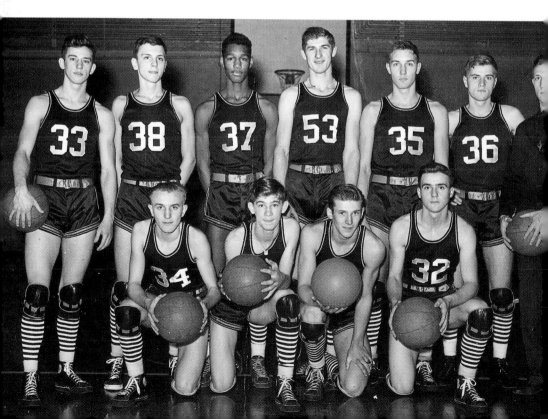

Nevertheless, the players who showed up for the Bears basketball practice wanted to be there as much as I wanted to be their coach.

Nellie even pitched in by washing the team's socks and athletic supporters with a special softener she bought. This may not sound like much (or maybe it does), but it was very helpful because stiff socks can cause blisters. A coarse athletic supporter creates its own kind of problems.

A good teacher or coach must not only understand others, but himself or herself as well.

Because our early morning practices overlapped with first-hour study hall at South Bend Central, I received permission for the boys to make it up at the end of the day. In effect, the players were kept after school to study. Unintentionally, this worked to my advantage because their girlfriends weren't allowed in the study hall, got bored waiting, and went home. I think it's one of the reasons my players were generally good students—they got to study without any distractions.

While my Bears never won a state championship, the teams always had good seasons and several times won regional or sectional titles. Along the way I improved at working with faculty, students, and alumni who occasionally disagreed with me and also got better at not just listening, but actually "hearing" what others said.

But I had a lot to learn. A good teacher or coach must not only understand others, but himself or herself as well. One of my single biggest mistakes and regrets as a coach happened at South Bend Central because I was still figuring this out.

NO SMOKING

I had an absolute rule forbidding the use of tobacco. Any player who broke it was automatically cut from our team with no second chance, no excuses—"Clean out your locker and don't come back."

One of our best players, I won't mention his name, broke the rule. This young man was on his way to an athletic scholarship and a good college education when I caught him smoking. In my mind, a rule was a rule—I dismissed him without remorse or a second thought. The effect on the youngster was traumatic, and it soon became apparent. He dropped out of South Bend Central without graduating, and never got the college education and a chance for a better future he deserved. Instead, I found out later, his life became a series of low-paying jobs when it could have been so much more.

A reprimand or a suspension would have accomplished what I wanted, but in those days I lacked the maturity and experience—wisdom—to do that. Everything was in black-and-white terms with no middle ground, no compromise, and no attempt to understand the bigger picture (as Coach Curtis had done when I stormed off the court during practice). "Be more interested in finding the best way, not just in having it your way," is good advice. Unfortunately, I didn't learn this in time to help my player.

How would it make you feel to hurt someone like I hurt him? Profound responsibilities come with teaching and coaching. You can do so much good—or harm. It's why I believe that next to parenting, teaching and coaching are the two most important professions in the world.

Common sense, an ability to read human nature, and good judgment are among the most valuable assets a teacher and coach can possess—much more important than just ABCs or x's and o's. I worked to improve in these areas, but it was not easy. We need to recognize the

difference between a principle that matters, and a rule or regulation that doesn't justify capital punishment. We need to be open-minded yet minding to those things that matter. We need to couple firm discipline with fairness and reason, understanding and compassion. It took me too long to get a handle on what is the appropriate balance for all of this.

BE MORE INTERESTED IN FINDING THE BEST WAY, NOT JUST IN HAVING IT YOUR WAY.

I quote this little poem occasionally as a reminder not to go overboard on enforcing rules and regulations:

Stubbornness we deprecate,
Firmness we condone.
The former is my neighbor's trait,
The latter is my own.

I wish I had taken this message to heart sooner as a coach and teacher.

PAYING THE BILLS

During this time I also found part-time work with Harcourt Brace Publishing. Because they knew my teaching salary was low and that I was working fifty- and sixty-hour weeks, an executive would contact me regularly about working full-time for the company. I'd get a phone call, usually at the end of the school year, asking, "Mr. Wooden, are you about ready to make a change?" It was almost as if they knew how cold it was in our basement locker room at the YMCA on those January mornings. I'd politely decline, but then accept assignments on various editing projects, usually English textbooks.

Our second child, James Hugh Wooden, arrived just as I completed a big editing job for seventy-five dollars (which was a lot of money). When the company found out about the birth of our son, they sent a gift set of encyclopedias to welcome the new arrival.

They also gave me something that reflected how I felt about parenting, coaching, and teaching—which in so many ways are alike. Printed on a special card were a couple of verses from a poem called "The Little Chap Who Follows Me":

A careful man I want to be.
A little fellow follows me;
I do not dare to go astray,
For fear he'll go the self-same way.
I cannot once escape his eyes.
Whate'er he sees me do, he tries.
Like me he says he's going to be,
The little chap who follows me.

That little chap's name was Jimmy, the new member of the Wooden household. That poem still hangs on the wall of my den.

WE COULD STAY FOREVER

Our years in South Bend were wonderful—I was making a living doing what I loved, everyone was healthy, and we loved the city and our friends there. Additionally, teaching high school students had its own great rewards. Students are more impressionable and receptive—more open to being taught—in high school than they are later when they go off to college. A high school student is more likely to ask, "How?" In college, the student is more likely to ask, "Why?" I preferred to spend time teaching *how* rather than explaining *why*.

Looking back, even with all the subsequent attention at UCLA, there is no doubt in my mind, nor in Nell's, that we would have been totally happy and completely content staying put in South Bend, Indiana—raising our family with me teaching high school baseball, basketball, and English.

THE WAR CHANGES EVERYTHING

World War II is the reason we left and ultimately arrived at UCLA. After serving as a lieutenant in the navy from 1943–46, I returned home to find things in the South Bend school system had changed.

The only time Nell ever got furious with me was when I enlisted without telling her.

Coaches who had gone overseas and fought were, in some cases, being denied their jobs when they got back from the war. Yes, they were given other duties, but not the jobs they had been doing previously—namely, coaching. I was treated OK, but I didn't like what I saw happening to friends—other coaches—throughout South Bend. The treatment was so wrong that I wanted to get out of the entire system and find a job elsewhere.

Kokomo and Marion High Schools were interested in hiring me, but when Indiana State Teachers College in Terre Haute called, I listened and accepted their offer of $3,500 a year. Our family packed and we headed south. I was about to become a college basketball coach, but our enthusiasm was greatly diminished by the simple fact that we loved South Bend, Indiana, and the Bears.

8

THE SYCAMORES, SPEED, AND SEGREGATION

At Indiana State Teachers College in Terre Haute, I was stepping into the sizable sneakers of my Martinsville High School mentor, Coach Glenn Curtis. He was now a Hoosier legend—four state championships, as many as any Indiana high school coach had ever won—and the success continued at Terre Haute. His decision to coach in a new professional basketball league was not welcomed by Sycamore fans.

I immediately ruffled feathers by replacing many of his returning squad, including starters, with players I had coached at South Bend Central— Jimmy Powers, Don Kozoroski, Bill Jagodzinski, Dan Dimich, Bob Smith, Lenny Rzeszewski, and others. They already understood the fast-break style that I'd been taught by Piggy Lambert,

IMPLE DEMONSTRATION
TO PROVE MY POINT.

much different from the deliberate ball-control pace of Glenn Curtis and most other coaches of the day.

To me modern basketball was about speed, and like Piggy Lambert, I taught speed. "Move, move, move!" I'd shout, and then, "Faster, faster, faster!" Always quick and pressing and shooting—not carelessly, but taking it to the opponent. I called it positive aggression, and it occasionally caused us to make mistakes, but I was somewhat tolerant of an error made in that circumstance.

Coach Lambert had preached at Purdue, "The team that makes the most mistakes will probably win." I couldn't go quite that strong, but I believed if you were not making some mistakes, you were not doing anything. You need to *do* something to make things happen. "I'd rather have a 50 percent shooting average and score 100 points, than a 100 percent shooting average with 50 points," I explained to players. "The former has mistakes. The latter is perfect. I'll take mistakes over perfection for a hundred points—but not a lot of mistakes." (Coach Lambert's point was that the "doer" will make mistakes. Mistakes of commission, to a point, are accepted, but not mistakes of omission—that is, the mistake of not doing anything.)

"Be quick, but don't hurry," I'd instruct. "But be quick!" Quick was good. Hurrying was careless. I wouldn't tolerate careless mistakes, and warned, "Please don't make a second mistake because you're thinking about the first."

Initially, my change to a fast-break style with some glaring miscues didn't go over well in Terre Haute, especially with some of Coach Curtis's returning players. When we lost our first game to Fort Sheridan,

51–49, the resistance remained. For those who hung on to Coach Curtis's slower style of play, I offered a simple demonstration.

I asked our fastest player, Bobby Royer, to demonstrate how quickly he could move the ball up the court dribbling at top speed. We were standing next to each other under the basket, each of us holding a basketball. I blew the whistle, and Bobby took off dribbling as fast as

The Sycamores went to Madison Square Garden. Coach Piggy Lambert disagreed, but it was my call.

he could—and he was very fast. At the same instant, I threw my basketball to a player standing at the far end of the court. Bobby had dribbled approximately three yards when my pass reached the fellow standing under the other basket.

I blew the whistle and said, "Bobby, I think you were holding back just a little. Let's do it again, but this time please run as fast as you can." The second time he managed to go four yards before my pass arrived up court. To emphasize my point, the player who caught the ball, Jimmy Powers, made a casual layup.

"Fellas," I asked, "is there anyone here who still doesn't understand the fastest way to move a basketball up the court?" I saw a lot less dribbling and a lot more passing after that demonstration.

As I was working my way through the season, a creative student manager also tried to help me out. He wanted to circulate a petition for changing the name of the school—removing the word *Teachers* from Indiana State Teachers College. The young man felt that having *Teachers* in the name hurt our image and kept superior athletes away.

I explained nicely that I was a teacher and proud of it. I also explained that teachers were what the school was producing, not basketball players, and that I wouldn't be working at a place where turning out basketball players was the goal. After our talk, he decided not to circulate his petition.

The Sycamores finished with an 18–8 record, won our conference, and received a postseason tournament invitation to the 1947 NAIB national play-offs (National Association of Intercollegiate Basketball, later the NAIA). It was held in Kansas City, Missouri, and drew top teams from all over the country. But it produced an unexpected crisis for me.

The invitation carried with it a prohibition against black players. Like most people, I had been raised to believe segregation was wrong. "You're just as good as anybody," Dad would tell me, "but no better than anyone." Not better, but just as good—equal. Now as a coach, I was being asked to participate in segregation, a system based on the belief that some people are better than others. That was not what Dad taught me.

THANKS, BUT NO

Clarence Walker, a student-athlete from East Chicago, was a ninth or tenth man on the Sycamore team and worked hard, attended class, and was a good fellow. He also was black. The NAIB wanted me to tell Clarence to stay home while his fellow team members—who were a team in part because of him—enjoyed the benefits of what the *team* had achieved. Clarence's reward was to be left behind while

the Sycamores traveled to the big tournament in Kansas City. How do you do something like this to a young man? I quietly turned down the invitation.

The following year it happened again. We finished 27–7 and had attracted nationwide attention with our so-called racehorse style of basketball. When the invitation from the NAIB arrived, it was difficult to say no quietly—we would be one of the main attractions in Kansas City.

Nevertheless, I informed the committee that the Sycamores would not attend and gave my reason. They offered a compromise: "Walker can play in the games, but he must not be seen publicly with the team. He must stay in a private home away from the other players. He must not attend publicity functions with the Sycamores." I felt this humiliation was worse than leaving Clarence behind in Terre Haute. The answer was easy: "No."

Then I received a call from the NAACP (National Association for the Advancement of Colored People) suggesting I reconsider, "If Clarence agrees to the impositions, he will become the first black player ever permitted to play in a national college basketball tournament." I talked it over with Clarence, who then talked it over with his parents in Chicago. They all agreed that it was worth it, so I accepted the NAIB's invitation to play in Kansas City starting March 8, 1948. It had some unexpected consequences for his white teammates, who got a taste of Jim Crow.

Traveling by bus through segregated towns on the way to Kansas City meant we encountered some restaurants and diners that wouldn't serve Clarence, which meant I wouldn't allow them to serve his teammates. Instead, we stopped at poorly stocked roadside stores where my assistant coach, Ed Powell, would buy some hard rolls and cold cuts. There were some hungry boys on that bus by the time we got to Kansas City, but they had learned in a small way what it's like to be considered inferior and undesirable simply because of your skin color. Of course, this was something Clarence already understood.

Other coaches objected to the segregation policy of the tournament just as I did. I wasn't acting in a vacuum. However, years later an all-black team won the event, and I would guess a few coaches never forgave me for fielding the first team that included a black student-athlete.

We had a wonderful tournament, but lost in the finals to Louisville 92–70, a well-coached and superior team. For the Sycamore players, fans, and me, however, it had been a very rewarding season both on and off the court.

The success we enjoyed brought offers from other colleges as far away as California. My goal, however, was to get back into the Big Ten where I'd played as a Purdue Boilermaker.

Among others, the Minnesota Gophers—a Big Ten team—Boston University, and the UCLA Bruins were interested. Minnesota was my first choice, but I flew out to California on a DC-3 to talk about the UCLA job. When I returned, I told Nellie, "We're going to Minneapolis if they'll let me pick my own staff." This was the only unresolved issue I had with the Gophers.

On Monday, Minnesota officials said they'd let me know by six the following Saturday night, April 17th. UCLA said they'd call at 7 P.M.

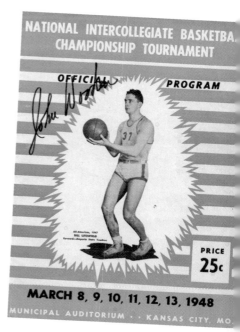

NATIONAL INTERCOLLEGIATE BASKETBA. CHAMPIONSHIP TOURNAMENT

OFFICIAL PROGRAM

PRICE 25¢

MARCH 8, 9, 10, 11, 12, 13, 1948

MUNICIPAL AUDITORIUM · · KANSAS CITY, MO.

to find out what I was going to do. After several days of discussion Minnesota relented, and on Saturday afternoon they decided I could pick my own staff. At exactly 6 P.M. they picked up the phone to call with their good news. But the line was dead. All telephones lines in the Minneapolis–St. Paul area had been knocked out by a freak April blizzard, and phone service wasn't restored until 7:15 P.M.

By then I had talked to Wilbur Johns, UCLA's athletic director, and accepted their offer. "Minnesota never called back," I told Wilbur.

NAME ORGANIZA

Johnny Wooden Resigns

Will Take Position as Head Coach At UCLA; Leaves State after July 1

John R. Wooden, head basketball c̲̅ ̲̅ ̲̅ ̲̅ ̲̅ rector announced Tuesday that he would r̲̅ ̲̅ re an accept the position of head basketball ̲̅ ̲̅rsity o California at Los Angeles. He will con̲̅ ̲̅ positio until July 1. At UCLA he will repla ̲̅ ̲̅ho wi become athletic director.

"I deeply regret leaving State at th ̲̅ortuni such as the one UCLA offered does ̲̅ ̲̅ry day
decl̲̅ ̲̅en ask
for ̲̅ his le
ing.

WOODEN TAKES NEW SPOT

JOHNNY WOODEN.
Coach of Indiana State basketball team resigned today to go t
University of California July 1.

U̲̅ ̲̅t enr
me̲̅ ̲̅000, is
ca̲̅ ̲̅, and
con̲̅ ̲̅ol ha
had its first graduating class in ̲̅
It is a member of the Pacific C
conference along with such no
schools as University of Sou
California, California unive

Dr. Compton Scheduled As Convo Speaker

Chancellor Arthur H. Compton, Nobel Prize winner and noted atomic ̲̅ ̲̅t of Washington university

Fifteen minutes later Nellie answered the phone, and it was Minnesota on the line telling me the job was mine.

It was too late. I had agreed to go to California.

After completing my duties as coach of the Sycamore baseball team that spring, Nellie and I packed up our family for the trip west. One of the things I packed with pride was the Pyramid of Success.

Success is not something that

others can give to you.

9

THE PYRAMID

DEFINING AND ACHIEVING SUCCESS

As a brand-new teacher in 1932 at Kentucky's Dayton High School, I was greatly troubled by the pressure parents put on children in my English classes. Anything less than an A or a B was viewed as failure even if the youngster had worked hard—to the best of his or her ability.

In sports, I had learned painfully that sometimes you're defeated—outscored—even when you do your best. Twice, even though we gave it all we had, my Martinsville Artesians lost the championship game of the Indiana state high school tournament. And yet we were neither losers nor failures. The Indiana State Sycamores had been outscored by Louisville in the 1948 NAIB championship game and yet had every right to be proud of their performance. At UCLA we were on the short end of the score 148 times, including twice in the final seconds of the Final Four. But on those occasions when the Bruins prepared and played to near their potential, I considered them a success. Was there something more I could require of them? I think not.

Likewise, I believed any student in my English class who did his or her best but received a B or a C shouldn't be judged a failure nor made to feel ashamed. Perhaps other students had worked just as hard but were simply better at the subject.

WHAT IS SUCCESS?

I had not always felt this way. At Martinsville High School, my history teacher, Mr. Scheidler, asked students to write an essay on the question, What is success? My answer was the same as everyone else's in class—namely, fame, fortune, and power, or an A in Mr. Scheidler's class.

But over the years my feelings changed. As a teacher, coach, and parent I wanted to come up with a better way than grades or a winning percentage for judging success and failure—something that was both fair and very productive. I remembered what Dad had told me, "Don't worry about being better than somebody else, but never cease trying to be the best *you* can be." At Dayton I began thinking that success should be measured along the lines he described—by one's effort in the classroom, in sports, or in life.

At about this same time, I read a very insightful poem while I was waiting for a haircut in a Dayton barbershop. It gave me some additional perspective:

At God's footstool to confess,
A poor soul knelt and bowed his head.
"I failed," he cried. The Master said,
"Thou didst thy best, that is success."

That summed it up pretty well for me—do your best, that is success.

Thus in 1934, after careful consideration for the exact wording, I wrote down my personal definition of success. It is the standard by which I have judged myself and those under my supervision: "Success is peace of mind which is a direct result of self-satisfaction in knowing you did your best to become the best that you are capable of becoming."

I wanted those under my supervision to understand the highest goal and greatest reward exist in the effort they make to achieve their potential. This is what Cervantes was getting at when he wrote, "The journey is greater than the inn." For me the "journey" is my effort, and it is

Success is peace of mind which is a direct result of self-satisfaction in knowing you did your best to become the best that you are capable of becoming.

truly much greater and more rewarding than the "inn" provided by fame or fortune, grades or victories. So I began teaching this idea to English students, student-athletes, and parents. It wasn't easy then, and it's harder now.

Our society tells us all that matters is, "Who's number one?" By this standard, most of us are losers. I think the opposite is true: we all have the potential to be winners. We may or may not drive a bigger car, get a better grade, or score more points than someone else. But for me the "score" that matters most is the one that measures your effort—and ultimately, only you know the score.

BUILDING THE PYRAMID

Soon enough I realized that I had only addressed half of the issue: defining success. As a teacher I understood the need for showing students exactly how to achieve it. That's when I began the Pyramid of Success—a combination of personal qualities and values that I believe are intrinsic to making the effort to reach your potential as a person.

I remembered that Coach Curtis had used a drawing of a ladder, where each of its rungs represented something he viewed as important for achievement. Well, I couldn't use a ladder, but then I realized a pyramid was a better device for representing important qualities and characteristics, as well as how they fit together and complemented one another.

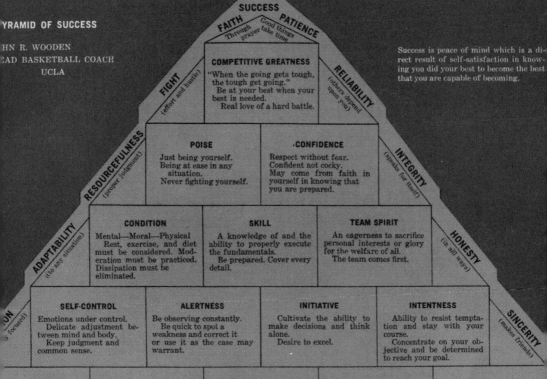

PYRAMID OF SUCCESS

JOHN R. WOODEN
HEAD BASKETBALL COACH
UCLA

SUCCESS

Success is peace of mind which is a direct result of self-satisfaction in knowing you did your best to become the best that you are capable of becoming.

FAITH — *Through prayer*

PATIENCE — *Good things take time*

COMPETITIVE GREATNESS
"When the going gets tough, the tough get going."
Be at your best when your best is needed.
Real love of a hard battle.

FIGHT *(effort and hustle)*

RELIABILITY *(others depend upon you)*

INTEGRITY *(speaks for itself)*

POISE
Just being yourself.
Being at ease in any situation.
Never fighting yourself.

CONFIDENCE
Respect without fear.
Confident not cocky.
May come from faith in yourself in knowing that you are prepared.

RESOURCEFULNESS *(proper judgment)*

ADAPTABILITY *(to any situation)*

HONESTY *(in all ways)*

CONDITION
Mental—Moral—Physical
Rest, exercise, and diet must be considered. Moderation must be practiced. Dissipation must be eliminated.

SKILL
A knowledge of and the ability to properly execute the fundamentals.
Be prepared. Cover every detail.

TEAM SPIRIT
An eagerness to sacrifice personal interests or glory for the welfare of all.
The team comes first.

SINCERITY *(makes friends)*

SELF-CONTROL
Emotions under control.
Delicate adjustment between mind and body.
Keep judgment and common sense.

ALERTNESS
Be observing constantly.
Be quick to spot a weakness and correct it or use it as the case may warrant.

INITIATIVE
Cultivate the ability to make decisions and think alone.
Desire to excel.

INTENTNESS
Ability to resist temptation and stay with your course.
Concentrate on your objective and be determined to reach your goal.

INDUSTRIOUSNESS
There is no substitute for Worth while things come from hard work and careful planning.

FRIENDSHIP
Comes from mutual esteem, respect, and devotion.
A sincere liking for all.

LOYALTY
To yourself and to all those dependent upon you.
Keep your self-respect.

COOPERATION
With all levels of your co-workers. Help others and see the other side.

ENTHUSIASM
Your heart must be in your work.
Stimulate others.

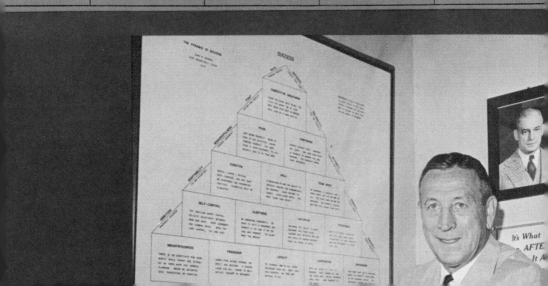

I worked on it for a period of about fifteen years and didn't finish until 1948, just before we left Indiana State Teachers College for California and UCLA. Here is the Pyramid of Success that I have taught from that day forward.

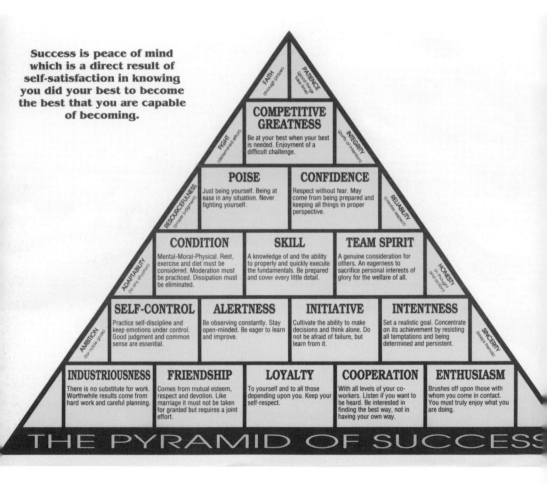

Success is peace of mind which is a direct result of self-satisfaction in knowing you did your best to become the best that you are capable of becoming.

FAITH (through prayer)

PATIENCE (Good things take time)

FIGHT (determined effort)

COMPETITIVE GREATNESS
Be at your best when your best is needed. Enjoyment of a difficult challenge.

INTEGRITY (purity of intentions)

RESOURCEFULNESS (proper judgment)

POISE
Just being yourself. Being at ease in any situation. Never fighting yourself.

CONFIDENCE
Respect without fear. May come from being prepared and keeping all things in proper perspective.

RELIABILITY (creates respect)

ADAPTABILITY (to any situation)

CONDITION
Mental-Moral-Physical. Rest, exercise and diet must be considered. Moderation must be practiced. Dissipation must be eliminated.

SKILL
A knowledge of and the ability to properly and quickly execute the fundamentals. Be prepared and cover every little detail.

TEAM SPIRIT
A genuine consideration for others. An eagerness to sacrifice personal interests of glory for the welfare of all.

HONESTY (in thought and action)

AMBITION (for noble goals)

SELF-CONTROL
Practice self-discipline and keep emotions under control. Good judgment and common sense are essential.

ALERTNESS
Be observing constantly. Stay open-minded. Be eager to learn and improve.

INITIATIVE
Cultivate the ability to make decisions and think alone. Do not be afraid of failure, but learn from it.

INTENTNESS
Set a realistic goal. Concentrate on its achievement by resisting all temptations and being determined and persistent.

SINCERITY (keeps friends)

INDUSTRIOUSNESS
There is no substitute for work. Worthwhile results come from hard work and careful planning.

FRIENDSHIP
Comes from mutual esteem, respect and devotion. Like marriage it must not be taken for granted but requires a joint effort.

LOYALTY
To yourself and to all those depending upon you. Keep your self-respect.

COOPERATION
With all levels of your co-workers. Listen if you want to be heard. Be interested in finding the best way, not in having your own way.

ENTHUSIASM
Brushes off upon those with whom you come in contact. You must truly enjoy what you are doing.

THE PYRAMID OF SUCCESS

10

WELCOME TO CALIFORNIA
A RUDE AWAKENING

California was almost frightening to Nell, Nancy, Jimmy, and me. I was a farm boy at heart, and our whole family had loved small-town life in Indiana. Suddenly we were far from friends, family, and loved ones in a city with too much traffic and not enough weather. Christmas felt like summer, and there was no winter, spring, or fall. We had loved the changing of seasons, but in California the season never seemed to change.

Adding to our sense of loneliness and loss came very sad news one day: my father, Joshua Hugh Wooden, had passed away—the man who had given me the compass I followed in life was gone.

A sad day—Mom, my brothers, and I say goodbye to Dad.

Living in Los Angeles was not an easy adjustment. Socially, I often didn't fit in, because I was a teetotaler who didn't smoke or swear and on many occasions was made to feel uncomfortable about it. On top of everything else, the traffic scared us. One day while I was driving very cautiously on the Pasadena Freeway, I looked at Nell and said, "What in the world are we doing out here, honey?" She was kind enough not to remind me that it was all my doing.

I was barely able to make a down payment on a modest home in Mar Vista, California, by cashing in my retirement plan at Indiana State Teachers College. I couldn't, however, keep up the mortgage payments with my $6,500 UCLA salary; I had to find a second job. So during the summers of my first four years as head coach of the UCLA Bruins, I started work at 6:30 A.M. as a dispatcher for Edgemar Dairy Farms Processing in Venice, California.

For three hours each morning I issued delivery orders to Edgemar truck drivers carrying butter, milk, and eggs to local stores. After they made their rounds, I'd call in the next day's orders, sweep up the office, and head to UCLA.

WELCOME TO UCLA

During the basketball season, my assistant, Ed Powell, and I would start the coaching part of my day by filling up two buckets with hot water and mopping down the court of the gymnasium.

On my first day of practice as the new head basketball coach of the UCLA Bruins—Friday, October 15, 1948—here's what greeted me on that freshly mopped

court: a group of young fellows who'd been picked to finish dead last in the Pacific Coast Conference and looked like they should. Many wore old T-shirts from home, mismatched and frayed trunks, and sneakers needing replacement. Even the basketballs were worn out. This was due, in part, to the fact that basketball was a poor cousin to the football program and was funded accordingly.

I'm ashamed to admit didn't believe in our tea at first. I never made th mistake again.

1948–1949
PAC. COAST SO. DIV. CHAMPIONS

UCLA's record the previous year was 12–13 overall and 3–9 in the conference (a tie for last place), and during the preceding two decades, the Bruins had only four winning seasons.

Our gymnasium—nicknamed "B.O. Barn" because of the foul smell caused by poor ventilation—was a dingy, crowded place with only two baskets. Private team meetings were impossible, and practices were conducted in the noise and commotion of Greco-Roman wrestlers and trampoline gymnasts working out at the same time. It was a raucous hodgepodge not conducive to good teaching.

The fans who showed up for games didn't even fill the modest roll-out bleachers in the gymnasium. This in spite of the fact that it held less than half as many spectators—about two thousand—as the one at Martinsville High School. In fact, I felt the Artesians could probably have given these players a pretty good scrimmage.

There was no question in my mind that if someone had produced a magical ticket back to Terre Haute, South Bend, or Dayton, Nell and I would have packed up the kids and returned—happily. But to my great astonishment the 1948–49 UCLA Bruins gave me what is perhaps the single most satisfying year of my entire teaching and coaching career. The young men also taught me a good lesson.

For whatever reasons—perhaps the losing years—Eddie Sheldrake, George Stanich, Ralph Joeckel, Carl Kraushaar, and the other boys were willing and eager to accept my coaching. They immediately took to the fast-break style I taught—the same one Piggy Lambert had taught me at Purdue.

Our speed caught slower West Coast opponents by surprise—Stanford, California, Washington State, Loyola, University of Southern California (USC), Fresno State, and others. To the amazement of almost everybody, the Bruins won the final 12 games of the regular season and finished the year with a 22–7 record—champions of the Southern Division of the Pacific Coast Conference. Even though we lost to Oregon State in the conference's title game, it was truly an unforgettable, almost stunning, season.

The team surprised me and we surprised opponents as well as fans, alumni, and the media. While I was pleased at the turnaround, I wasn't happy that I had been among the skeptics. The shoddy uniforms, the rundown men's gym, UCLA's losing reputation, and the opinions of others affected me and lowered my expectations of the boys. It was a betrayal of those who looked to me for leadership.

The lesson I learned in watching these young men work hard and improve through the season was valuable: before casually discounting the potential of any individual or team, give them a chance to succeed—give them your sincere belief and full support. I was slow in

The Christmas tree in my UCLA office had some unusual "decorations."

doing that, a cautious doubter. I corrected this mistake by late January of that first season at UCLA and never repeated it again. It served me well in 1964 when UCLA—not even ranked among the top fifty teams in preseason polls—won the NCAA national championship.

My second season at UCLA saw more improvement—24–7 overall and champions of the Pacific Coast Conference—and produced UCLA's first-ever invitation to the NCAA basketball tournament. The excitement this created in fans is hard to overstate. My first twenty-four months at UCLA had seen a remarkable turnaround in the university's basketball program. The Bruins hadn't put two winning seasons back-to-back since 1930 and 1931. No subsequent national championship gave me more satisfaction than what occurred in that first year at UCLA. Everyone said the Bruins couldn't win, but they did—and the next year they did it again.

Before casually discounting the potential of any individual or team, give them a chance to succeed—give them your sincere belief and full support.

That first season also produced perhaps the most glowing and over-written review I've ever received. The 1948–49 yearbook, the *Daily Bruin,* said the following: "Taking over only an average group of boys, Jovial John proceeded to bamboozle the world of sports by producing the scrappiest aggregation of lanky lems ever to set foot on a Bruin hardboard-patch." Even this hyperbole, however, didn't change the fact that Nell and I still had a strong yearning for the Midwest.

YOU CAN'T GO HOME AGAIN

As it turned out, Purdue had a yearning for me. My mentor, Piggy Lambert, had retired and the school was offering his position as Boil-ermaker's head basketball coach for nearly twice my UCLA salary, a new car each year, a better gymnasium, a perpetual five-year contract

with built-in pay raises, a country club membership, a home on campus, a large life-insurance policy, and a full-time assistant coach—something UCLA would not provide. It was almost unimaginable what Purdue offered.

I hurried to a meeting with Athletic Director Wilbur Johns and Bill Ackerman, the graduate manager of the Associated Students Union—my boss—and politely requested that I be allowed to forgo the third and final year of my UCLA coaching contract. Wilbur and Bill reminded me that it was John Wooden who had insisted on a three-year deal. They had reluctantly agreed to this demand with the expectation that I would fulfill my part of the bargain.

Nell loved our games, but eventually they took a toll.

Of course, they also liked the turnaround UCLA had made in basketball. From their perspective, changing coaches was ill-advised. From my perspective, they were being self-serving at my expense. I would never sign another three-year contract again. Deeply disappointed, I reported back to Nell and promised we'd simply wait one year until my contract was up, then take the offer from Purdue and move back home where we belonged.

One year later Purdue didn't make an offer. Nor did Minnesota or anyone else. By then it really didn't matter, because the family was starting to like California—Nancy Ann and Jimmy didn't miss freezing weather and had new friends, Nell enjoyed seeing the kids happy and even tried some golf, and I increasingly saw basketball talent all around me in Los Angeles.

California was going to be our permanent home.

11

GLORIOUS WITHOUT GLORY

THE EDUCATION OF A COACH

I believe the truth of this axiom: "It's what you learn, *after* you know it all, that counts." But I also believe your knowledge and experience reaches a point, in time, when you know what you're doing—or should.

I taught basketball at UCLA for fifteen years before the Bruins won a national championship in 1964. This decade and a half gets little attention, now or then, but it was a most valuable period because it was when my coaching and teaching reached a maturity. The foundation for ten NCAA national basketball championships was put in place during this time as I refined and expanded on what my father and three mentors had given me. (Of course, I also tried to learn from coaches on the other side of the court—Kentucky's Adolph Rupp, California's Pete Newell, and others.)

Coach Warriner at Centerton Grade School taught me that arrogance, selfishness, and envy are unacceptable in a player. This was my introduction to the concept of team spirit—the absolute necessity for an individual to put the group's welfare ahead of his or her own interests (such as an interest in shooting all the time). Like Mr. Warriner, I used the power of the bench on fellows who were slow learners—just as he used it on me. I wanted everyone, starters and nonstarters alike, to understand that "the star of the team is the team."

THE BENCH HELPS SIDNEY BECOME AN ALL-AMERICAN

As a sophomore in 1969, Sidney Wicks could have been a starting forward for virtually any school in the country. But he was not a starter at UCLA, because he was having difficulty with my concept of team play.

He was too concentrated on having the ball and shooting before he'd look for the pass. This is damaging because, among other reasons, teammates soon stop working to get open for a shot, as they know they won't get the ball. It then becomes every man for himself, and the team is destroyed. Thus Sidney wasn't a starter.

He would say to me, "C'mon Coach, you know I'm better than either start-

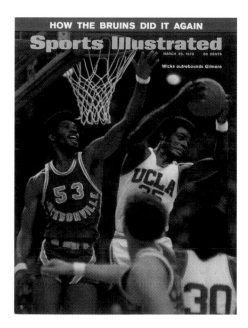

ing forward." I'd nod and reply, "I know it, you know it, and they know it. So it's a shame they're going to remain starters until you get the hang of playing as part of a team."

Sidney did get the hang of it by his junior year and became the best all-around forward in the country for the next two seasons, an All-American both years, and a crucial part of two national championship teams in 1970 and 1971. The bench, in my opinion, helped make this possible.

DISCIPLINE WITHOUT ANGER

I was comfortable being a disciplinarian, but did not want to be an ogre. Therefore, when discipline was required, I tried to dole it out in a manner that was firm but fair, with no emotionalism or anger attached. Anger prevents proper thinking and makes you vulnerable.

For example, Bill Walton would argue vehemently that he had a right to wear long hair. I would remind Bill—very firmly, but without anger—that I also had a right—namely, the right to choose who was on the UCLA team. Bill would think about it for a moment, then get on his bicycle and pedal down to the Westwood barbershop for a trim. (People have asked me if I would have suspended Bill for long hair. My answer: "Bill thought so.")

It never got personal, because the purpose of criticism or discipline is not to punish, embarrass, or ridicule, but to correct and improve. It is very difficult to antagonize and teach at the same time. For this reason I avoided criticizing a player or the team at the end of practice, because the effect lingers and is magnified. I violated this only on occasions when a serious jolt was called for: "A team must have leadership and I am the leader of this team. You needn't follow me blindly, but I do require that you follow me." Sometimes the youngsters needed to think about that message overnight.

I began concluding each practice on a fun note by running a drill that players liked. For example, I might designate one young man to make five free throws in a row at different baskets before the team was dismissed to the showers. The whole group would gather around to hoot and holler depending on the shooter's results. Of course, it also allowed that player to practice free throws under pressure, and I always picked someone who needed practice.

Later, when the dunk was outlawed, I allowed five minutes of dunking at the end of practice. The players had as much fun as if they were stealing cookies out of the coach's cookie jar because they knew I deplored dunking (and still do). All of this was an upbeat finish to our two-hour practices, which were so exhausting that occasionally players would tell me the next day, "Coach, I was too tired to change clothes before I went to bed last night." I was hoping this also meant they were too tired to cause any mischief.

LITTLE THINGS MAKE BIG THINGS HAPPEN

Coach Glenn Curtis's disassembling of the game of basketball into small parts and perfecting the parts increasingly became a fetish with me. I saw that the identification and perfection of relevant details—the fundamentals that Coach Curtis and Coach Lambert practiced but others neglected or thought foolish—were major factors in outscoring other teams. I grew to love seeing little things done well, and I believe it is probably the greatest secret to success.

I was enthusiastic about beginning another season—my fifth—at UCLA.

For instance, on the first day of practice I personally showed players how to put on their sweat socks to prevent blisters. This may sound trivial or foolish, but a blister causes pain, pain causes a distraction, and a distraction can cause a turnover. Socks, put on correctly, may prevent a turnover, which in turn may win a game. What if that game is for the national championship?

LITTLE THINGS DONE WELL IS PROBABLY THE GREATEST SECRET TO SUCCESS.

I don't like sloppiness on or off the court. Players not only were well-groomed and dressed neatly on road trips, but also put towels in the towel basket and not on the floor, picked up soap and turned off their showers, and put gum and candy wrappers in the wastebasket. I insisted on this because sloppiness in one area breeds sloppiness in another.

Equally important, I did not want a player to think student managers were there to pick up after them. Believing you're so important that a fellow student should follow behind and clean up your mess contributes to an unhealthy ego. Controlling the egos of those under your supervision is one of a leader's great challenges, but it is crucial to creating a strong team of *selfless* individuals eager to sacrifice for the group.

I felt there was a connection between picking up after yourself and a healthy ego. It's a small thing, but if you do enough small things right, big things can happen.

TEACHING X'S AND O'S

This same obsession with perfecting details—that is, reducing mistakes and eliminating sloppiness—was applied to teaching players, individually and as a unit, the hundreds of specific interrelated movements required for correct passing, pivoting, dribbling, screening, shooting, blocking, receiving, and more. The formula I used to teach this is uncom-

If you do enough small things right, big things can happen.

plicated: explanation, demonstration, imitation—correction, when necessary—and then repetition, repetition, repetition, and more repetition.

"That's good. Now do it again, faster," was my constant call during practice, because I wanted to see near-perfect execution coupled with the most intense hustle. Some players told me the drills were often faster than actual games. The drills were usually no longer than ten minutes each, because players would lose intensity after that amount of time. I wanted them to be mentally aggressive—fresh—in their execution. (Drills were no shorter than five minutes each, because it required at least that much time for the lesson to have any effect.)

All drills—except free throws—had running as a by-product, whether it was shooting, playing defense, or rebounding. This was my method of conditioning players, rather than having them run laps or up and down steps tediously. If shooting or defending was involved, they didn't mind running.

INFORMATION ON THE RUN

Like Piggy Lambert, I moved up and down the practice court shouting out instructions and information to individual players—what to do and how to do it—rarely addressing the whole team, but instead one, two, or three players at a time.

There was no chitchat, no banter, no small talk. I did not hand out praise gratuitously; however, I praised nonstarters more than starters (nonstarters need encouragement, while starters are getting plenty off the court). And I rarely praised scorers in front of others, but openly complimented players who did the less glamorous tasks—rebounding, passing, blocking. I conducted practice in an intense, businesslike, and serious manner without being overly stern, grave, or sour. I wanted players to have fun without being funny.

Finally, I tolerated no horseplay during a practice, because the way you practice is the way you play. It wastes precious time, distracts others, and creates a lackadaisical environment.

METICULOUS ORGANIZATION

Organization, which I define as knowing what must be done and doing it in the allotted time, became a strength of mine. It resulted, I believe, from necessity—throughout most of my career I held numerous jobs simultaneously. I had to learn how to budget my time or I'd run out of it. Additionally, teaching English at Dayton High School and South Bend Central had forced me to learn how to use each minute of the hour very efficiently.

So I started planning practices down to the exact minute on three-by-five-inch cards and in notebooks, so there was never any standing around waiting for something to happen. Planning the practice took longer than the practice itself. I would keep my notes and refer back to

This is my first drawing of the Pyramid of Success, which I took with me to California.

them from one year to the next. They showed me how not to waste time. I had 120 minutes to conduct practice, and each minute had value to me and our team. In order to maximize our short time together, my assistant coaches also had to know exactly what they were doing—and they did: Denny Crum, Gary Cunningham, Jerry Norman, Frank Arnold, Doug Sale, Ed Powell, and more.

I adopted and modified Coach Curtis's use of poems, and tacked maxims and mottos, precepts and worthy phrases on the bulletin board: "Discipline yourself and others won't have to," "Respect every opponent, but fear none," "The best way to improve your team is to improve yourself," "Do not mistake activity for achievement," "It is amazing how much we can accomplish when no one cares who gets the credit," and "Time spent getting even would be better spent getting ahead."

Some might say these are corny expressions, but I believe the messages they contain are true and have a positive impact on those who read them.

TOURNAMENT TROUBLES

During those early years, even though UCLA won the conference or division title six times, we lost in the first round of the NCAA tournament in each of our three appearances—1950, 1952, 1956. This disturbed me because the Bruins seemed to play at a different and lower level.

I gradually—too gradually—recognized that I was the source of the problem. My preparation for a tournament game was hurting our team—new plays were added, practices were even more rigorous, and I tried to work everyone into the rotation.

DISCIPLINE YOURSELF AND OTHERS WON'T HAVE TO. RESPECT EVERY OPPONENT, BUT FEAR NONE. THE BEST WAY TO IMPROVE YOUR TEAM IS TO IMPROVE YOURSELF. DO NOT MISTAKE ACTIVITY FOR ACHIEVEMENT. IT IS AMAZING HOW MUCH WE CAN ACCOMPLISH WHEN NO ONE CARES WHO GETS THE CREDIT. TIME SPENT GETTING EVEN WOULD BE BETTER SPENT GETTING AHEAD.

But by 1962, important adjustments had been made. I began concentrating just on those things that got us into the tournament—adding nothing new. I stopped overworking players, so they'd be fresh. I also focused my attention on those young men who were going to play the majority of minutes in the tournament games. These were crucial additions to my coaching that occurred before 1962 and our first trip to the Final Four.

COACH LAMBERT'S TEAM UNITY

Most important, I shared Coach Lambert's belief in teaching young men how to play as a team, to perceive themselves as a unit and be selfless in their sacrifice to it: "The strength of the pack is the wolf and the strength of the wolf is the pack."

UCLA team members were taught that teammates were responsible for their success: "It takes ten hands to make a basket." They were instructed that whenever a Bruin scored, that player was to give a nod or a wink to the assisting teammate. One player asked, "Coach Wooden, what if he isn't looking at me?" I said, "Don't worry. I'll be looking."

Very seldom was a player allowed to have a basketball to himself during warm-ups or practice shooting. Basketball is not a solo game, and shooting baskets alone creates the false impression that it is. Also for this reason, I viewed managers as full members of the team, just as those players who got little actual playing time were UCLA Bruins and not subs, benchwarming Bruins, or second-stringers.

There was no "first" team or "second" team. A team begins to deteriorate when the leader allows some of its members to be viewed as second- and third-class citizens by others. There were starters and nonstarters, yes, but there were no class divisions associated with this. In fact, I instructed those on the bench to use this time productively and study what those in the game were doing. They were also told to "be prepared, because if your chance comes and you're not ready, it may not come again."

I also started to recognize that the five best players don't necessarily make the best team. Of course I'd prefer to have my five most talented student-athletes starting a game, but to become a starter, the player needed to combine talent *with* teamwork. Talent alone would not get you on the starting team. This was the lesson that Sidney Wicks (and many others) learned on his way to becoming a great All-American.

AS SIMPLE AS ONE, TWO, THREE

My coaching mentors were by my side in spirit during this time. By the early 1960s, I had a devotion to the following three principles and knew how to teach them:

1. **Condition.** Supreme physical condition accompanied by mental and moral conditioning is foremost. Performance diminishes immediately when condition is insufficient.

2. **Fundamentals.** Players must have the ability to properly execute the basics of the game instantaneously without having to stop and think. This concept is taught through relentless repetition of details (and I was the one who determined which details would be perfected).

3. **Team Spirit.** Most important of all, each young man must be willing and *eager* to sacrifice personal glory for the good of the group. "One for all and all for one" is a phrase that still sends a chill down my spine. The college teams that bring me so much pride are those that demonstrated the highest level of team spirit—the 1948 Indiana State Sycamores and the 1949, 1964, 1970, and 1975 UCLA Bruins. They exhibited a unity that even Coach Piggy Lambert would have admired.

CONDITIONING FUNDAMENTALS TEAM SPIRIT

THE BIGGEST DIFFERENCE

While other coaches also stressed some of those principles, I differed greatly from them in what I didn't stress; namely, I never talked about winning or beating an opponent. In fact, I rarely mentioned the opponent's name. (One player joked that just before games our manager would go to the lobby and buy a program in order to know who the team was playing that day.)

"Let them worry about us," was my philosophy. My job, and the team's job, was to get *us* as close to being as good as we could get. The final score would be a by-product of that effort. Dad's advice was at the core of my coaching: "Don't try to be better than someone else, but never cease trying to be the best *you* can be. You have control over that. The other you don't." As the years passed, I was determined not to let those things I couldn't control detract from those things under my control.

All of the preceding principles came from Earl Warriner, Glenn Curtis, and Ward "Piggy" Lambert. And, of course, my head coach was Joshua Hugh Wooden, a man whose interest in the game was minimal.

No one who understands basketball has ever accused me of complicated play-making or intricate strategizing. What I taught was as simple as one, two, three. But, without being self-congratulatory, I believe I taught "one, two, three" fairly well.

THE ADVANTAGE OF CHARACTER

During those early years, some schools in the Pacific Coast Conference (later the Pac-8, now the Pac-10) would admit players who couldn't meet the higher academic requirements of UCLA. Suddenly, excellent athletes who couldn't get into our university were coming right back into town as opponents—and beating us.

At first I was frustrated and then very angry. I complained to anyone who cared to listen about the unfairness of this situation. Slowly, very gradually, I came to view the situation as an advantage. Perhaps I was rationalizing on a grand scale, but it seemed that many of these better players were not always better people. Too often they were mediocre or poor students who also attracted problems off the court. Furthermore, what I saw on the court suggested they weren't inclined to be good team players. Not all of them, of course, but enough so that I noticed.

Character is at the center of what I consider necessary for an individual to be a team player.

I concluded—begrudgingly, because all coaches hate to see talent go elsewhere—that UCLA wouldn't have been as good a team with many of these excellent but academically ineligible players.

Now you might wonder about the connection I see between character and basketball teams or any kind of team. Character is at the center of what I consider necessary for an individual to be a team player. A person of good character tends to be more considerate of other people—of teammates, for example. A person with character tends to be more giving and sharing with others—with teammates during a game, for example.

I believe in passing the ball whenever appropriate and possible. I don't believe a person who is selfish—selfishness is a character issue—would be as willing to pass the ball to a teammate who might then make a basket. You may laugh. Is hogging the ball a character issue? Yes, I believe it reveals an aspect of character. I wanted most of our baskets to come from a pass. A selfish player doesn't like to pass the ball.

Furthermore, conditioning—physical, mental, and moral—is crucial to performance. I believe conduct between practices has more to do with conditioning than with anything I can devise for players during practice. Does a player of good character dissipate his or her physical, mental, and moral resources between practices? Perhaps, but less likely than his or her counterpart.

A person of character works better with others—with teammates, for example—day to day, game to game. Such a person is more polite, more courteous, more in tune. And most of all, he or she is most eager to do what's best for the team. I repeat: *eager* to do what's best for the team.

Whatever talent an individual possesses, character helps that person use his or her ability to serve the team.

Goodness gracious, sakes alive, these are powerful personal qualities regardless of context—basketball, business, or anything else. For me, it's pretty clear: whatever talent an individual possesses, character helps that person use his or her ability to serve the team. While I can't prove that a person of good character has more potential as a team player, I can prove that's the person I want to coach. A scientist might find otherwise, but scientists don't make a living teaching young men and women how to play basketball.

GETTING BACK TO DAD

When I came to this realization, it also helped modify my own behavior. I had started to drift away from some of the principles—the code of conduct—Dad had taught me, including his two sets of threes.

Increasingly, I was given to complaining or making excuses when things didn't work out. For example, at Dayton High School I initially complained about the Green Devil players. Later, B.O. Barn, lack of fan interest, academic standards, and a limited budget became easy targets. The self-pity I had when I wasn't released from my UCLA contract was another example. Here was something totally of my own doing, but I was upset with Wilbur Johns and the Associated Students Union for the situation.

My complaining, whining, and making of excuses subsequently ended. Those good players who were good people helped me accomplish this. Those good players who weren't such good people helped me recognize it.

Learning should be a lifelong process and I hope I've continued to listen and learn, but by 1962 much of my coaching philosophy was in place. Obviously, I had no clue as to what lay ahead. If you'd asked me, "John, do you think you'll win ten national championships?" my honest answer would have been, "I will be very grateful, extremely grateful, if we win even one."

12

CHAMPIONSHIPS

THE BEGINNING OF THE BEGINNING

On Saturday night, March 21, 1964, at Kansas City's Municipal Auditorium, UCLA played Duke for the NCAA basketball championship. The Bruins outscored the Blue Devils 98–83 to win our first national title. Many view this as the beginning of UCLA's so-called dynasty— ten national championships in the next twelve years. But in my opinion, the beginning began two years earlier.

In 1962, UCLA reached the Final Four for the first time ever. We did it with a group of young men *Sports Illustrated* described as having "no height, no center, no muscle, no poise, no experience, no substitutes, and no chance." It suggested that early in the season UCLA was not tough enough to "mash a mango."

My own opinion—based in no small part on the lesson taught to me by the 1948–49 Bruins—was more optimistic. I told reporters with a wink, "We're not quite as bad as we look." I was correct. By the end of the year, some were calling us the Cinderella Team.

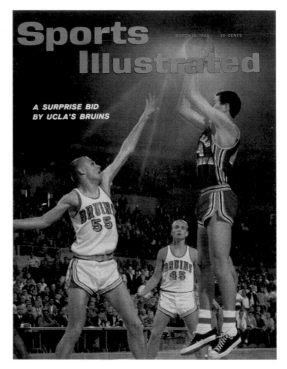

Others were "surprised," but I hadn't forgotten what my first UCLA team had taught me.

Walt Hazzard, Fred Slaughter (our six-foot-five so-called midget of a center), Gary Cunningham, Peter Blackman, John Green, and everyone else kept working hard and improving despite losing 7 of their first 11 games. Their effort produced dramatic results as the season progressed, and UCLA won 14 of the final 18 games, became Pac-8 champions, and went to the NCAA tournament.

In the regionals at Provo, Utah, the Bruins outscored Utah State and then Oregon State to advance to the Final Four in Louisville for the first time. This was quite a surprise to most basketball fans around the country. Our 72–70 loss in the last seconds of the the Final Four semifinals to the defending and eventual champion, Cincinnati, provided great evidence of how one can "lose" and still win.

THOU DIDST THY BEST, THAT IS SUCCESS

No team I've ever coached got closer to achieving their full competency, their full potential, than those 1962 UCLA Bruins—neither the amazing group of boys I coached my first year at UCLA nor the team that won UCLA's first national championship in 1964.

Gradually, UCLA basketba
was gaining fans. Maybe tha
the point of this publicity sh
of me stuffing two footballs
into a wastebasket.

Cincinnati's narrow victory was most painful—it still hurts—but it provided me with the greatest satisfaction and peace of mind. I believe we came within a whisker of winning the national championship in 1962, but Cincinnati's best was slightly better than ours. In my eyes, that could not make Walt, Fred, John, Peter, Gary, and the other Bruins losers—the final score can never make you a loser when you've done your best.

Moreover, I have pride in that Final Four loss to Cincinnati. It also reinforced a central concept in my philosophy; namely, a coach is a teacher and one of the most important lessons to be taught is that players are successful when they do their best—even when the final score goes against them. This team had done just that.

I wanted to win—that is, outscore the opponent—every single game I was ever involved in. Of course I did. But my deep belief is that the score is a by-product of something much more important: effort.

SCORING IS THE BY-PRODUCT OF SOMETHING MUCH MORE IMPORTANT: EFFORT.

When you put forth your best effort, you can hold your head high regardless of the by-product called "the final score." That's why I've always taken greater pride in the effort than in the score. Following the loss to Cincinnati, the 1962 Bruins could walk out of the locker room in Louisville with their heads held high—and they did. Their coach joined them in that walk.

If you trace the origins of the subsequent ten national titles, this team is a good place to begin because two starters—Walt Hazzard and Fred Slaughter—moved on to play a central role in the 1964 UCLA national championship, but they moved on with the addition of a powerful ally: the full-court press.

THE POWER OF THE PRESS

Prior to the start of the 1962–63 season, my assistant coach, Jerry Norman, got me thinking about reinstating the press, primarily because of two new arrivals: Gail Goodrich, a tremendous competitor, and Keith Erickson, perhaps the best pure athlete I've ever coached. Keith also had size and quickness. He was the perfect fifth man for the system and would become the on-court "dictator" of the press—basically the on-court captain of the system.

I had used the press at South Bend Central and Indiana State, but had never stuck with it at UCLA, because it's difficult to teach and requires both great athleticism and supreme conditioning. Frankly, I also thought most college teams could easily figure out how to get around it. I was wrong about that.

The goal of the press is to create mistakes, that is, more and more errors until the opponent's offense starts to break apart. You create these mistakes by applying a stifling and aggressive defense up and down the court—starting, of course, the instant the opponent tries to in-bound the ball under their own defensive basket. Done right, it can upset the opponent psychologically. Coach Forrest Twogood of USC said it was like being locked up in a casket for six days.

The press becomes almost insidious and takes advantage of human nature. An opponent who makes a mistake tends to hurry and try to correct the mistake. This often can cause another mistake; one compounds another, and suddenly you see players dribbling off their toes, passing into the stands, or throwing the ball into the opponent's hands.

Of course, when this happened, UCLA tried to capitalize on the errors by scoring points quickly. Soon I saw games where there would be a scoring burst—the media called it the "Two-Minute Explosion"— where we'd outscore the other team by 10 or 15 points. In fact, in the finals of that 1964 national championship—the year after we began installing the press—Duke was leading UCLA 30–27 midway in the first half when their offense started to break apart under our press. The Bruins scored 16 straight points in two and half minutes. Duke never recovered, and UCLA won its first national title.

1963 is when I committed to teaching and applying the full-court press. We lost in the NCAA regionals that year to Arizona State, but I had recognized during the season that we were on the verge of creating a kind of team unlike anything basketball had seen before. The combination of conditioning and execution with the Bruins' fast break and full-court press could be very destructive. In tandem, they would allow us to set the speed of the game—fast—which would ultimately give the team in better condition an edge. Conditioning, of course, was a priority I learned from Piggy Lambert at Purdue.

Knowing that every 1963 starter, now well-schooled in the press, would be returning in 1964—Walt, Fred, Keith, Gail, and Jack—led me to write the following poetic prophecy prior to the 1964 season:

With every starter coming back
Yes, Walt and Gail and Keith and Jack
And Fred and Freddie and some more
We could be champs in sixty-four.

Twelve months later, UCLA won its first national basketball championship.

Better than a trophy, blue ribbon, or gold medal.

13

THE FIRST NATIONAL CHAMPIONSHIP
UNDERSTANDING PEOPLE

A good parent, teacher, coach, or leader—and really they're all the same—must understand human nature. No two individuals under our supervision are alike and shouldn't be treated as if they were. I didn't recognize this when I started out.

By the time the 1964 season arrived, I'd been at it for three decades and my understanding of human nature had improved. This became an important factor in the Bruins' first national title and those that followed, because the difference between a good team and a great team is usually a leader's ability to understand others—human nature—and teach accordingly.

A good parent, teacher, coach, or leader—and really they're all the same—must understand human nature.

Three of the group's most talented players, Walt Hazzard, Gail Goodrich, and Keith Erickson, all brilliant athletes, were very independent souls and completely dissimilar. Treating them alike would have been counterproductive. I had

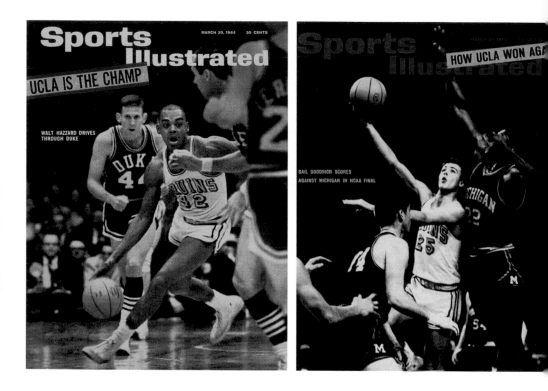

always advised players that if a coach "bawls you out," consider it a compliment. It means the coach cares about you and your importance to the team; otherwise, the coach wouldn't bother. Not all players are able to take this advice to heart, however; so I learned to adjust my teaching accordingly.

Gail Goodrich was very high-spirited but had to be worked with in an almost gentle manner. Given a sharp rebuke, he'd go into a shell and almost sulk. Nothing would be accomplished. I had to tone down

COLLEGE BASKETBALL **THE TOP 20**

Sports Illustrated

DECEMBER 6, 1965   35 CENTS

THE UCLA PRESS: HOW TO BEAT IT

my critical comments about his technique or whatever and offer instructions in a softer way.

As a result, I'd try to combine a compliment with a criticism. I might have said, "Gail, oh boy, if you could just cut to your right like you cut left, that would really be something to see." And he'd do it just like that. Earlier on in my teaching career, I would not have been wise nor patient enough to do this.

His teammate Keith Erickson enjoyed horseplay and fooling around during practice, which I didn't permit. Unlike with Gail, however, I was able to be very direct—almost rude—with Keith, and it would bounce off him like water off a duck's back. But he'd get the message without taking it personally.

Once, during UCLA's pregame warm-ups at Kansas State, I was standing on the sideline talking to a reporter when I noticed Keith horsing around down at the other end. I immediately excused myself and started walking briskly toward him—very displeased. He caught sight of me and stopped right away, but I kept walking straight at him. When

I was about six inches away, I hissed under my breath, "Keith, it's a good thing I decided to count to 15 on my way over here, because if I'd counted to 10, as I usually do, you'd be on your way back to California." He nodded, said, "Sorry, Coach," and continued the warm-up correctly, no hurt feelings. He just liked to have a little fun—occasionally at the wrong time—and I had to calm him down.

Walt Hazzard was totally different from either Gail or Keith. A big compliment would go in one ear and out the other, as if I hadn't spoken a word. If I made him mad at me, however, the results were amazing. Walt's attitude would become almost defiant when I criticized him, as if to say, "Well, Wooden, I'll show you!" And he usually did because he was so good.

One problem, however, took a while to fix. Walter was an extraordinary player, but one who liked to use fancy moves such as dribbling behind his back or between his legs. Some called him "East Coast" because the style of play back there was more given to showboating.

This show-business type of play was unacceptable to me because it drew attention away from the team and onto the player. Additionally, it was not fundamentally sound and provided little advantage that I could see. But when I tried to stop Walt's entertaining moves, he would become upset and think I was trying to hurt his game.

This was serious for me. Walt was (and is) a good person and was probably the team's foremost basketball player. I wanted to work with him in a way that was productive and achieved my goal—namely, getting him to cut out the flamboyance. Furthermore, I knew if I allowed one player to violate a clear rule, others would soon be breaking rules they didn't like.

The last seconds of the first championship.

So I called Walt's father, Reverend Walter Hazzard, in Philadelphia, and explained that I was going to take some hard measures: I was going to bench his son. Reverend Hazzard told me to do whatever was necessary. After I benched Walter, he immediately called his dad and announced that he was quitting the Bruins and moving back home. I am told that Reverend Hazzard replied, "Son, don't come back here because my door will be locked."

I can't say that Walter stopped all of the fancy stuff, but he toned it down enough for us to have a workable compromise. Compromise was also something I had to learn along the way.

Let me also tell you this: even without the flamboyance, Walter was just a delight to watch, perhaps the greatest passer I've ever coached—and I love passers. Additionally, because of his eagerness to pass the ball, his teammates worked feverishly to get open. Walt was a perfect example of what happens when a player is more interested in helping the group than in boosting his own statistics.

Another player on that first championship team who tested me was Jack Hirsch, the only fellow I've ever coached who called me John. In my early years, I wouldn't have tolerated this informality, but by this time I somehow felt that if it made Jack feel good, what was the harm?

All of the preceding examples and many more resulted from my attempt to get better at understanding human nature—mine as well as other people—so I could be a more effective teacher. Understanding human nature is absolutely crucial to a leader's success.

The 1964 team is dear to my heart, perhaps my favorite. Like a first child, a team that brings a first national championship is very special, even more so with this group because of the circumstances. After all, at the beginning of the year they were not even ranked among the top fifty teams in the country.

Comparatively speaking, they were also the shortest team to ever win a national championship—our center, Fred Slaughter, was only six foot five. My message to them was simple: "I don't care how tall you are, I care how tall you play." And Walt Hazzard, Jack Hirsch, Gail Goodrich, Keith Erickson, Doug McIntosh, Kenny Washington, and Fred—our short center—played tall. They were the first team to efficiently execute the full press that I had begun teaching at South Bend Central High School. Additionally, they practiced in the chaotic conditions of the men's gym and played all "home" games on makeshift courts elsewhere, because in 1956 the fire marshal declared that UCLA crowds were too big for the gym—it was a fire hazard. Equally pleasing to me was the way they worked together on the court—like a hand in a glove. Their togetherness on court has never been surpassed by any group of players I've coached; they were a single unit, a real team.

All of this didn't impress most of the critics, however. On the Saturday morning of the championship game, I sat in the lobby of the Muehlebach Hotel in Kansas City writing a little birthday note to my daughter, Nan. As I did so, many folks stopped by to offer their kind regards and condolences that although the Bruins were a capable team, Duke, our highly regarded opponent in the finals that night, was a tall team. And tall teams win. "Nice try, Wooden," was what I sensed. Although UCLA had won every single game that season, the boys were still viewed as almost lucky to be in the finals. This burned me up.

This is the starting five from the first national championship team. They looked like champions should look.

That evening, Walt, Keith, Jack, Gail, Fred, Doug, and the rest of the young men outscored Duke 98–83 for UCLA's first national basketball championship. Ironically, it happened in the same Kansas City Municipal Auditorium where my Indiana State Sycamores had lost to Louisville in the finals of the NAIB championship in 1948.

The following year, 1965, UCLA outscored Michigan 91–80 to win its second straight NCAA championship. Suddenly, or so it seemed to some, I was an overnight success with two national basketball titles.

The truth is that it took about fifty years—going all the way back to our farm in Centerton, Indiana, when my dad nailed a tomato basket with the bottom knocked out to the hayloft our barn.

14

J. D. MORGAN

A HELPING HAND

On the day I was hired as UCLA's new head basketball coach in 1948, Wilbur Johns, the University's athletic director, assigned me the task of budgeting and scheduling everything related to the Bruins' basketball program. It was a complicated and time-consuming job.

I spent hundreds of hours detailing, arranging, and invoicing travel, lodging, and dining as well as scheduling opponents and ordering most of our supplies, including uniforms, shoes, socks, basketballs, and almost everything else. All of this on a very small budget. On road trips our trainer, Ducky Drake, and I would even search for cheap restaurants to save money on team meals because hotel meal prices were always higher. All of this was a distraction from coaching and teaching. It also alienated a few of the hotels that we stayed at, and some didn't want us back.

This all changed starting in 1963 with the arrival of the new athletic director, a big, bold, outspoken fellow by the name of J. D. Morgan. While he had little to do with UCLA's NCAA championships in 1964 and 1965, he recognized how important they could be and he seized on it. In the spring of 1965, here's how he signaled his commitment to the future of UCLA basketball.

THROWING AWAY MY HARD WORK

One afternoon I was busy in my office poring over the details of the projected budget and schedule for the upcoming year. The desk and a connecting table were stacked up with piles of papers full of numbers, names, and timetables.

Suddenly, towering over me was J. D. Morgan, who asked in his deep, rolling voice, "What are you doing there, John?"

Looking up from my work and irritated by his interruption, I said, "Mr. Morgan, I'm trying to get the budget request put together for next year. Could we talk later?"

Without saying a word, J.D. leaned down with his arms outstretched and scooped up almost everything on my desk—papers, notebooks, receipts, and all the material I had worked so hard on for weeks. Then he slowly walked over to the corner of my office and dumped it into, and around, a large, metal wastepaper basket. I was speechless.

J.D. came back to my desk and said, "John, you just take care of getting that team ready to play basketball. I'll handle the rest." From that moment—April, 1965—I could focus completely on teaching basketball. It was as if he had given me another assistant coach named John R. Wooden. We had our differences from time to time, but J. D. Morgan knew what he was doing.

PAULEY PAVILION

The new athletic director also understood the advantage of having a modern basketball facility. When I arrived at UCLA in 1948, it had been with the indication that the men's gymnasium would be replaced within three years. Fifteen years later, it still hadn't been done. Morgan recognized what Pauley Pavilion would provide—more revenue, easier recruiting, and greater fan support. What I understood better than J.D. was how much more productive my practices would become.

By 1964, he also had heard about Lewis Alcindor, Jr.—the best high school player in the country—who was deciding where to go to college when he graduated from New York's Power Memorial Academy in 1965.

J. D. Morgan cleared my desk of everything unrelated to teaching basketball.

Michigan, St. John's, Oklahoma, and other fine schools were all interested. J. D. Morgan let young Lewis know that Pauley Pavilion, a five-million-dollar, state-of-the-art gymnasium would be completed by the time he enrolled at UCLA.

Lewis and his parents, Cora and Ferdinand, were attracted by UCLA's academic reputation and environment, but I have no doubt that Lewis Alcindor would not have attended our school if the old men's gym and various city college facilities had been his "home" court. It would have been a downgrade from his high school days.

A player is a success only when he does his best in service to the team.

In my opinion, J. D. Morgan got the job of building Pauley Pavilion done. In the process, he also made me a much more effective coach and teacher.

HOW DID UCLA WIN ALL THOSE CHAMPIONSHIPS?

I'm probably no better at self-analysis than anyone else, but when I'm asked how players under my supervision won ten national championships in twelve years, here's the best answer I can give. I don't rate myself too high as a "game" coach, but I was among the best when it came to conducting practice. And practice is where a championship is won.

Also, I did have a sizable knack for recognizing talent and knowing how to use talented athletes—whether tall or short—within a system I was very good at teaching. (Few people besides coaches and sportswriters recognize that the only constant in our championship teams was quickness—some players were tall, some were short, but all were quick.)

If I had a "technique," it was my ability to get players to share my belief that a player is a success only when he does his best in service to the team; this is only possible with extreme effort in all areas. I defined many of those areas in the Pyramid of Success.

Importantly, J. D. Morgan's assumption of budgeting and scheduling duties let me coach full-time. And when he facilitated the construction of Pauley Pavilion—completed in June of 1965 just before Lewis arrived on campus—it not only made practices extremely productive, but also made UCLA more appealing to potential student-athletes.

J. D. Morgan's contribution was significant.

THE HARDEST VICTORIES

However, those first two national championships—1964 and 1965—made it all possible. Because they were achieved (1) under the near-hardship practice conditions of the men's gym, (2) with comparatively short teams who had no "home court," and (3) at a time when UCLA had no reputation for winning an NCAA basketball competition, I can honestly say they were more difficult to achieve than the next eight NCAA championships combined. There's no question in my mind about that.

However, once the pieces were put in place—and J. D. Morgan played a part in it—UCLA was on the verge of being an ongoing force in college basketball.

That's the best I can do in explaining how the so-called basketball dynasty happened.

15

THE AGE OF ALCINDOR

When I first saw Lewis Ferdinand Alcindor, Jr., now Kareem Abdul-Jabbar, I was simply amazed, not just with his height, seven foot two, but even more with his extraordinary demeanor. Lewis had the bearing of an eagle. He also reminded me so much of my own father, Joshua Hugh Wooden.

SELF-CONTROL AND POISE ARE FUNDAMENTAL TO ACHIEVING SUCCESS.

This may sound impossible because two men couldn't appear to be more different. One was white, the other black; one stood under six feet tall, the other over seven feet; one was a plain Midwest farmer, the other a superstar from New York. But they shared a most valuable quality: Joshua Hugh Wooden and Lewis Alcindor, Jr., both possessed such

My father and Lewis (Kareem Abdul-Jabbar) shared a most extraordinary quality. Both had the bearing and poise of an eagle.

powerful self-control and poise. I so greatly admire this and believe it fundamental to achieving success. Without it, how do we resist the temptations that pull us off course?

IGNORING THE COMMON ASSUMPTION

When Lewis chose to attend UCLA with its brand-new Pauley Pavilion, many felt my worries were over: after two national championships with short teams who practiced in an antiquated men's gym and played all "home" games at other local schools, things would now be easy— all I had to do was make sure the Bruins arrived on time for games. Lewis would take care of the rest.

I did not share this view. I kept in mind what had occurred at Kansas with Wilt Chamberlain, arguably an even greater and taller presence on court than Lewis. Kansas failed to win any championships. This was in spite of the fact that Wilt not only was slightly taller, but also had an arm span a foot greater than Lewis's (101 inches versus 89 inches). While no coach can win without talented athletes, not all coaches can win—even with talent. This has been demonstrated time after time.

WHILE NO COACH CAN WIN WITHOUT TALENTED ATHLETES, NOT ALL COACHES CAN WIN—EVEN WITH TALENT.

My perspective was that UCLA, with Lewis as a team member, had a great opportunity to win a national championship—our foot was in the door, so to speak. But I'd seen the door slam shut on many feet. For that door to remain open, I needed to help other members of the Bruins avoid two destructive attitudes: namely, jealousy and complacency.

Everything about Lewis demanded attention, and the media certainly supplied it. But Lewis's teammates were also talented—Lucius Allen, Kenny Heitz, Lynn Shackelford, Mike Warren, Curtis Rowe, Sidney Wicks, and others—and naturally wanted some credit. It wasn't easy.

During interviews after a game in which Lewis had scored 30 points, I would make a point of first complimenting a player who had made a valuable defensive play or set up a big basket. I tried hard to spread the attention around. But the reporters all wanted to talk to Lewis, and even

when they interviewed other players, the questions were usually about their tall teammate from New York. It's very difficult for a player who is working hard and making a contribution not to become upset—resentful—with this sort of treatment.

I would remind players that basketball was in some respects similar to the making of a movie. There was a star on the screen, but that star was helpless without a good script and costars, lighting and makeup experts, and all the other less recognized things that go into making a good movie. Without them, the star is meaningless. Our team, with Lewis, for example, had a star, but everyone's contributions were crucial. Lewis could do nothing without them. Then I would also remind them that a movie needed a director who was in charge of everything. I was the director.

IGNORE PROGNOSTICATIONS

Of course, when *Sports Illustrated* and other magazines predicted before the season began that UCLA would win the national championship,

Lewis and I were so different in many ways, but we were in total agreement that the team's best interests always came first.

complacency could have arisen within players. I told them, "If *Sports Illustrated* could predict the future, they wouldn't be wrong so often."

I told the Bruins that the only prediction they should believe is mine—namely, that we will work extremely hard *today* in practice. Nothing else is certain. Ignore predictions, both good and bad. Ignore outside criticism and praise, because they're usually wrong. Pay attention to one thing: the effort you make to help UCLA become the best team it can become.

To their credit, the young men on those teams with Lewis came close to doing just exactly that in winning three national championships. Lewis was superb, but he was superb because of his teammates—and his own desire to be a team player.

NEVER RUFFLED, NEVER RUDE

During his playing days at UCLA, Lewis was subjected to treatment I had never seen or heard before, even in the old Jim Crow days when we traveled to Kansas City with Clarence Walker for the NAIB tournament. Lewis bewildered people; his extreme height, color, athletic ability, and celebrity along with UCLA's dominance of college basketball at the time were just more than some could handle. Their comments reflected an opinion that Lewis was a spectacle, "some*thing*" rather than someone, an object and not a man.

On one occasion, a woman seeing Lewis for the first time pointed her finger at him and said within earshot, "Will you just look at this big, black freak!" as if he was a creature in the zoo. I explained to him the cruel comment—and others—was not racist, but simply shock, amazement, and awe. Lewis understood there was more to the woman's comment than just shock. He knew racism in a way I couldn't.

Through it all—the crude comments, the racial invectives, the physical pounding officials allowed opponents to give him, the discomforts of being extraordinarily tall (airplane seats, hotel beds, doorways, chairs, clothes, showers, cars, phone booths, taxis, classroom desks—nothing

Lewis was stoic under stress; calm in the most competitive situation.

was sized for a seven footer, and everything became a source of minute-to-minute aggravation)—Lewis Alcindor never complained, whined, or made excuses. This was true on small issues as well as big ones.

THE GAME OF THE CENTURY

On January 20, 1968, UCLA faced the Houston Cougars in what was being billed as the "Game of the Century." It was played in the Houston Astrodome, a building so big that I reminded players before we took the court, "Use the restroom now. You won't get back here until halftime. It's too far away."

At the time UCLA had won 47 consecutive games (the all-time record was 60) and ranked number one in the country, as well as was the defending NCAA champions. Houston was undefeated for the season and ranked second nationally. Additionally, each team would bring a reigning superstar to the game—Lewis Alcindor, Jr., and the Cougars' Elvin Hayes, or the "Big E," as the media referred to him.

In my opinion, the buildup surrounding this game became almost silly. In fact, it was initially called the "Game of the Decade," but promoters couldn't resist upgrading it. To me, the contest meant even less than a regular conference game, which affected standings, and it wasn't an NCAA tournament game where losing meant the season was over. But the hoopla was unlike anything basketball, and perhaps sports, had seen to that point.

In fact, some say it brought college basketball into the modern media age, because it was the first regular season game ever televised nationally in prime time. It was also played in front of the largest crowd—about 55,000—in the history of basketball, college or professional.

What went fairly unnoticed during the pregame hoopla was the fact that Lewis had trouble seeing the basket or anything else clearly, because he had been poked in his left eye during a game with California two weeks earlier. The Jules Stein Eye Institute determined that he had double-vertical vision caused by an abrasion on the iris of his eye—when he looked at a basketball hoop, he saw two or three of them stacked on top of each other.

Lewis sat out the two previous games, and if he hadn't insisted on giving it a try, I would have been very comfortable keeping him on the bench in the Astrodome. But he wanted to play. Competitors want to play even if it means going out there on crutches.

Subsequently, in the nationally televised Game of the Century, Elvin Hayes was spectacular, making 17 out of 25 shots, scoring 39 points, grabbing 15 rebounds, and blocking three of Lewis's shots. Then, with twenty-eight seconds left, Elvin made two pressure-packed free throws to win the game for Houston, 71–69. His picture was immediately on the cover of the next *Sports Illustrated*.

Lewis scored 15 points, the lowest total of his entire varsity career.

NO EXCUSES

After the game, Elvin suggested that his rival, Lewis Alcindor, Jr., wasn't so great after all, and that we now knew who really was the greatest college player in the country—Elvin himself.

Meanwhile, Lewis said nothing of his problem; he wouldn't allow it to be an excuse and didn't complain about his poor vision or how it had damaged his play. He simply moved on. But not before taping the cover of *Sports Illustrated* to the inside of his locker at Pauley Pavilion. It featured a picture of Elvin Hayes soaring over Lewis to score a basket.

Two months later, UCLA faced Houston again in the NCAA semifinals in Los Angeles. By then Lewis's vision was back to normal and so was his game. The Bruins outscored the Cougars, 101–69. Elvin scored 10 points. Afterward, there was no gloating or boasting from Lewis. His self-control and poise were amazing in both circumstances, winning or losing, excuses or not. This is quite admirable.

The following night, Lewis and the Bruins won their second straight NCAA championship, defeating North Carolina, 78–55. They would win a third consecutive title the following year against my alma mater, Purdue, 92–72. It was the culmination of what many predicted when Lewis Alcindor first arrived at UCLA.

A STARTLING INTRODUCTION

In his freshman year, 1965–66, Lewis and his frosh teammates—Lucius Allen, Ken Heitz, Lynn Shackelford, Mike Lynn, and others—played an exhibition game against the UCLA Bruins varsity, a team that had just won two consecutive NCAA championships (in those days, freshmen were not eligible for the varsity).

The contest was played with great fanfare because it was the inaugural game at the new state-of-the-art Pauley Pavilion. On Saturday night, November 28, 1965, one day after United Press International had picked the varsity Bruins to be number one in the nation, the freshmen defeated them 75–60 in front of over 12,000 fans. In fact, it would have been worse if their coach, Gary Cunningham, hadn't put the starting freshmen on the bench with four minutes to go.

The media saw a wonderful opportunity to ask an awkward question immediately following the game: "Coach Wooden, how do you feel about having your national championship team lose to the freshmen?" I replied, "The future looks good." And it did. As far as I was concerned, if the varsity Bruins had to lose to somebody, who better than my freshmen?

My pride in those years when Lewis was a member of the UCLA varsity and a superstar centered on the fact that his teammates never lost their identity and always played as a real team. I worked hard to achieve that, and so did they.

THE TEAM WITHOUT?

16

I refer to the 1970 UCLA Bruins—Henry Bibby, Steve Patterson, Curtis Rowe, Sidney Wicks, Andy Hill, Jon Chapman, Kenny Booker, Bill Seibert, Rick Benchley, John Vallely, Terry Schofield, and John Ecker—as the "Team Without." When people ask, "Without what?" I reply, "Not without what, without whom!" Lewis Alcindor, Jr., had graduated.

His departure brought hope to schools around the country that perhaps UCLA would finally get its comeuppance and fall back to the ranks of normal college basketball programs. This was something of an insult to the returning players—the Team Without—because many of them felt they had also contributed to the national championship in 1969; some had also been members of the 1968 championship team. Even though Lewis was popular with his teammates, all of them soon adopted an attitude of "We'll show you we can do it without the big guy."

Personally, I also had a new perspective. For three years with Lewis as a member of the team, outsiders simply assumed UCLA would win games and championships—automatically. With his departure, of course, that assumption disappeared. In a sense, after three seasons I

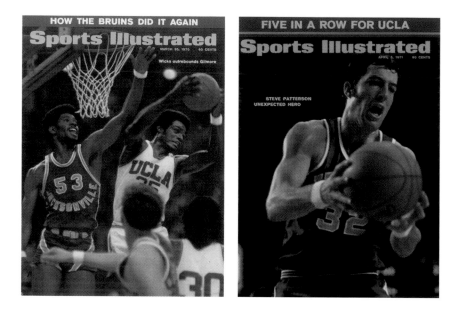

could once again coach to win rather than coaching "not to lose." It's correct to say that both the team and I felt we had a little something to prove.

Of course, with Lewis gone, some of our returning players found an opportunity to feel their oats a little and assert their new prominence and importance.

On October 14, 1969, the annual team picture day, one of our top players showed up with considerable muttonchop sideburns. I said, "There's a clippers in the dressing room. I want those trimmed off before the team picture is taken in fifteen minutes."

He said, "Coach, you haven't got the big guy this year. You need me."

I looked at my watch and replied, "You're right, I don't have the big guy this year and I won't have you either if you don't shave those sideburns off in . . . fourteen minutes."

A short while later, the full team posed for our official picture. Not a muttonchop was in sight. I'll admit this particular young man may have been having a little fun testing the waters a bit. I never begrudged a youngster who tested but then complied.

In the 1970 NCCA finals, Sidney, Curtis, Henry, Steve, and their teammates faced a sizable challenge. Jacksonville had three players taller than our center, six-foot-nine Steve Patterson: seven-foot-two Artis Gilmore, seven-foot Pembrook Burrows, and six-foot-ten Rod McIntyre.

After three years with Lewis towering over most opponents, UCLA was now in the position of being the "short" team—again. However, the Team Without played "tall."

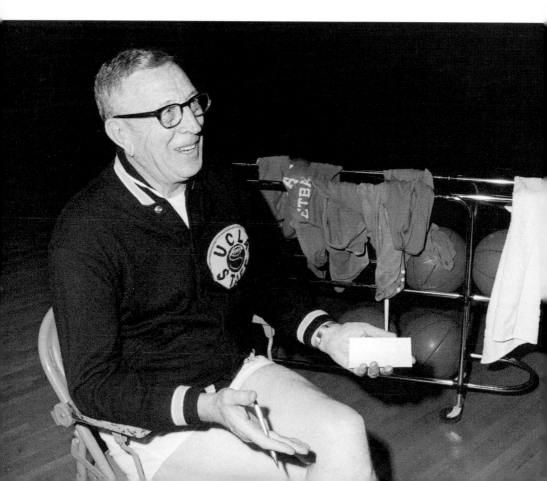

In the finals at Maryland's Cole Field House against Jacksonville University, Sidney Wicks scored 17 points, grabbed 18 rebounds, and dominated Artis Gilmore. And the Bruins outscored Jacksonville 80–69. The following year, 1971, Steve Patterson led the Bruins to another national championship with 29 points in the finals against Villanova. UCLA's "comeuppance" following the departure of Lewis Alcindor had extended the Bruins' string of consecutive titles to five— eight altogether—and the future looked promising.

Practice is where champions are created.

Getting ready to join the 1972 Bruins' varsity team following the upcoming departure of the Team Without was the "Team With."

With whom? Bill Walton.

Sidney, John, Steve, and the other members of the Team Without are very close to my heart, right next to the squad that won our first national championship in 1964. Both teams were discounted early (and late), both believed in themselves, and both worked so hard all the way. Most of us like to achieve difficult things that others say we can't do. Those teams did just that, and along the way gained my everlasting affection.

Whatever suggestions I made to referees were aided by my rolled-up program. Although I didn't use profanities, Lewis Alcindor claimed I was an expert at giving the "antiseptic needle."

You must *earn* the right to be proud

and confident.

17

THE WORLD OF WALTON

NEVER BEFORE OR SINCE

I am very fond of Bill Walton, but still shake my head in wonderment over his antics at UCLA in the 1970s. He seemed to lead two separate lives. One was the conscientious student, All-American athlete, and tall, talented team player. The other Bill Walton was an angry antiestablishment rebel who protested the war in Vietnam by lying down in the middle of Wilshire Boulevard, disrupting classes at the university, and closing the administration building. He was even arrested by police during one of his demonstrations.

How a nonconformist rebel conformed to my requirements for selfless team play is still a mystery to me; you'd have to ask Bill. What is not mysterious is this: if you took all the centers who ever played basketball, selected ten fundamentals you'd like a center to have, and graded each one on a scale from one to ten, I believe Bill Walton, when healthy, would be number one. It would be difficult to select anyone over him.

He might not have been the defensive player Bill Russell was or the offensive player that Wilt Chamberlain was, and he didn't have Shaq's enormous power or the deadly hook shot that Lewis had (no one does), but I rather feel Bill might rate right at the top overall.

THE WALTON YEARS

The three extraordinary seasons—historic, really—during which Bill was a member of our UCLA varsity squad, 1972–74, eventually caused a unique problem no coach has ever faced.

As sophomores, Keith Wilkes, Tommy Curtis, Greg Lee, and Bill Walton had a perfect 30–0 season and won the 1972 NCAA national championship against Florida State, 81–76. In the history of college basketball, only four other teams had ever achieved this (a perfect season and national championship). Two of those teams were from UCLA, 1964 and 1967—but those Bruin squads, for various reasons, had greater emotional constancy.

For example, the dominant presence on the 1967 squad was Lewis Alcindor. In 1972, it was Bill Walton. The temperaments of these two young student-athletes were vastly different. Both were hardworking, unselfish, and extremely competitive, but Lewis was quiet, contained, and self-controlled, while Bill was fiery, excitable, and visibly intense.

Reflecting Lewis's almost stoic style, the 1967 Bruins—Lynn Shackelford, Kenny Heitz, Bill Sweek, Jim Nielsen, and others—were much less disrupted by their perfect season and national championship, almost taking it in stride. The sophomores also benefited from the maturity of

March 23, 1973 · 6:00 p.m. · The Sports Arena · Los Angeles, California · $1.00

NCAA
National Collegiate Basketball Championship

23

National Collegiate Basketball Championship $1.00

NCAA
March 24 and 26, 1973
The Arena, St. Louis, Missouri

Sports Illustrated
UCLA'S RED-HOT REDHEAD
Center Bill Walton

UCLA **32**

Sports Illustrated
BASKETBALL'S SLAUGHTERHOUSE FIVE
Bill Walton Leads the Champs

UCLA **32**

43

Sports Illustrated
61 THE RECORD BUSTING WALTON GANG

UCLA **32**

34

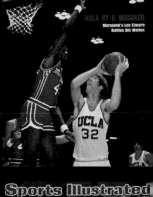

Sports Illustrated
UCLA BY A WHISKER
Maryland's Len Elmore Battles Bill Walton

UCLA **32**

BABE RUTH Part 2

Sports Illustrated
THIS TIME IT'S FOR KEEPS   UCLA vs. North Carolina State

UCLA **32**

24

BABE RUTH Part 3

Sports Illustrated
END OF AN ERA
N.C. State stops UCLA

THOMPSON **44**

52

34

Sports Illustrated
UCLA'S LOST WEEKEND

OREGON **50**

junior Mike Warren, perhaps as smart an on-court player as I've ever coached.

I feared otherwise for Bill and his fellow Bruins as time went on. Thus I tried to head off a potentially serious problem. Following their undefeated sophomore season and 1972 national championship, I met with Bill and the others—the media called them the "Walton Gang"— and said, "Fellows, I'm very proud of you and next year you're going to be even better. We'll know more about each other and what to expect from one another. The Bruins will be a much superior team because of it."

I looked around the room— they were pleased to hear this, smiles were everywhere and heads nodded in agreement—and then added solemnly, "But by the time you are seniors, you'll very likely become intolerable." Then I left the locker room.

What was I trying to do? Obviously, I was trying to *avoid* having them become intolerable, uncoachable, and overconfident.

As I predicted, they were an improved team the next season, perhaps as good as any I've ever

coached—30–0 and another NCAA championship. But as I feared, the "Walton Gang" would not be a better team the following year, their final season.

FAILING TO PREPARE IS PREPARING TO FAIL

As seniors, Bill, Tommy, Keith, Greg, and the others worked hard in practice and said all the right things, but I sensed something wasn't there. I felt at times the boys were just paying lip service to doing what they were supposed to do. My gut feeling was they were just too sure of themselves, going through the motions, flirting with complacency. A coach needs to take care of this, and I couldn't figure out how to do it, how to snap them out of it. The results confirmed my instincts.

After two NCAA championships and two perfect seasons during which they won 60 consecutive games by an average margin of 27 points, the Bruins suddenly had close games that shouldn't have been close, won some they shouldn't have won, had trouble holding leads, and seemed to lack the consistent on-court discipline of the previous two years.

Specifically, in the second game of their final season, 1973–74, we played Maryland at Pauley Pavilion where the Bruins had not lost a game in almost four years. We narrowly survived, 65–64.

Twelve games later we didn't survive—losing to Notre Dame in a game that snapped our 88-game winning streak. Could we have won? Maybe. With three and half minutes remaining, UCLA led 70–59. We did not score another point in the game, committed four turnovers, and

I shouted at the referee,
"What kind of a call was that?!" He answered,
"They liked it at the other end."

missed three tip-ins in the final six seconds. Notre Dame deserved to win and did, 71–70.

Then in the 1974 NCAA Final Four, we faced North Carolina State, a team we had easily defeated earlier in the season, 84–66. Now we lost, 80–77, in a double-overtime game that was ours to win. We did not.

Earlier in that same tournament, Dayton took us to triple overtime before we finally pulled it out. Dayton had no business taking us to a single overtime.

However, by almost any measurement, Bill and his teammates had a good year—a 26–4 record, a conference title, and a trip to the Final

There was a no-dunk rule during Bill Walton's college years. Subsequently, what he did under the basket was graceful and beautiful.

Four before losing to North Carolina State, the eventual champion.

But I had disappointment in the 1974 season, not because of close wins or losses or the 88-game winning streak being stopped by Notre Dame, but rather why these things occurred: the standard of success I believe in, and taught, had eroded within the team.

It is never simply a case of win or lose, because I do not demand victory. The significance of the score is secondary to the importance of finding out how good you can be.

WHAT COUNTS

For me it is never simply a case of win or lose, because I do not demand victory. What I demand—and that's exactly the word—is that each player expend every available ounce of energy to achieve his personal best, to attain competitive greatness as I define it. Victory may be the by-product, but the significance of the score is secondary to the importance of finding out how good you can be. This is only possible with ceaseless, not selective, effort toward that goal.

There is no shame in learning that someone else is better at doing something than you are. Shame is only justified when someone else is better because you failed to make the effort, 100 percent, to realize your potential. Shame is the appropriate response in that circumstance. So when a team or player decides—subconsciously or otherwise—to apply their effort selectively, against a tough opponent or in a game that really "counts," that player or team, in my opinion, has already lost (and often, but not always, the score will reflect it).

There should never be a need for me to give a pep talk to instill motivation. The motivation must come from the players' belief—deeply entrenched—that ultimate success lies in giving their personal best. More than anything, I wanted players to love the process of doing that.

Unlike a pep talk that might generate temporary enthusiasm, loving the process of working to be your best isn't temporary. When players truly believe this, giving them a pep talk so they can "rise to the occasion" is unnecessary; they've already risen to it. Now let the opponent try to rise to our level with a pep talk.

This belief is a pure and most powerful force. It has been and remains the source of my own motivation—not fame, fortune, or power, all of which can be taken away by others. No one can take away the effort you strive to make, under whatever circumstances exist, to be your best. This cannot be taken away by anyone but you.

The 1974 Bruins may have taken it away from themselves when they stopped striving to find out how good they could be. And I wasn't a smart enough coach to prevent it from happening.

PRIDE IN THE EFFORT MORE THAN THE RESULT

This is why I have such pride in our loss to Cincinnati in the 1962 NCAA Final Four. The Bruins' extraordinary effort during that season was nearly 100 percent and culminated in a wonderful, but losing, performance against Cincinnati. Conversely, I have no pride in UCLA's triple-overtime victory against Dayton in the 1974 NCAA tournament. The difference was in the quality of the effort by those under my supervision.

For me, how you play the game—and prepare for it—really does count. In fact, it counts most of all. Why? Because even winning can become routine. Striving ceaselessly to get better and better and better—and doing it—never becomes routine. At least not in my experience. Thus the effort should be the same whether you've won 88 games or lost 88 games in a row, whether you've won two consecutive NCAA championships or never heard of the NCAA. Effort. Effort. Effort. That's the highest and truest standard, and somehow it was compromised in the 1974 season.

To this day, however, I'm not sure how I could have fixed the problem these fine student-athletes faced: two perfect seasons and two NCAA championships before they were even seniors. Never in college basketball history had this been done, and it hasn't been done since. I believe many of these young boys simply couldn't conceive of how another team could beat them—even after it happened.

But it wouldn't have happened if I'd been able to teach them to have a greater love for the effort than the score—to believe that "Success is peace of mind which is a direct result of self-satisfaction in knowing you did your best to become the best that you are capable of becoming." I admit this is not easy to teach, and I was not able to do it in 1974. Here I am many, many years later still wondering what I should have done in the extraordinary circumstances of that unique season.

Someday another coach will have the opportunity to figure it out. I wish him or her good luck.

Goals achieved with little effort are

seldom worthwhile or long lasting.

18

A MEANINGFUL RECORD
A MEANINGLESS STREAK

UCLA won 88 consecutive basketball games between January 1971 and January 1974. In the process, the Bruins broke the previous record of 60 straight victories set by the University of San Francisco during the Bill Russell era.

When Notre Dame ended our streak in the 89th game, 71–70, on January 19, 1974, at South Bend, reporters were eager to know how I felt about UCLA's record-breaking run being stopped—how much did it hurt? To be honest, once the Bruins set the record of 61 straight wins, extending it for its own sake was meaningless to me. Breaking the record, however, was an accomplishment I am proud of.

The mark of a champion, I believe, is consistency of performance at your highest level under pressure. That's the apex, the highest block, of the Pyramid of Success.

The mark of a champion, I believe, is consistency of performance at your highest level under pressure.

The Bruins exhibited competitive greatness for two full seasons and portions of two others—an extraordinary length of time during which every single team we faced wanted to be the one who stopped UCLA. Crowds were naturally against us and rooting hard for the underdog, just as I do—unless the underdog happens to be my opponent.

APPROACHING THE RECORD

The oldest, most trite statement in sports is "one game at a time," but I didn't even take it one game at a time. I had learned to focus on what is immediately at hand, not something in the future. Setting a new record is in the future. Therefore, preparation, as usual, was my primary preoccupation and I tried hard to make it the team's. The boys never heard me mention the 60-game record in the days and weeks leading up to it—not tying the record, breaking the record, or anything about the record. They were being pestered about it everywhere they went, but their coach didn't bring it up.

However, when we outscored Loyola 87–73 to win our 60th consecutive game, deep down I was increasingly anxious; having now tied San Francisco's record, I wanted to break it.

The 61st game—to set a new college basketball record—was played on Saturday, January 27, 1973, at Notre Dame's Athletic and Convocation Center in South Bend, Indiana, where Nell and I had lived for almost fourteen years and still had many friends. As usual, she was with me for the game. I had great concerns about the contest because the Fighting Irish fans were boisterous and created an almost hostile

In twenty-one seconds, Notre Dame would end our 88-game winning streak.

atmosphere, which made it tough to win on their court. In fact, the last team to beat UCLA before our streak began was Notre Dame in the same arena in front of many of these same fans. I was mindful of the fact that it would be a great newspaper story if it was Notre Dame who stopped us from breaking the record.

Nevertheless, the Bruins—Bill Walton, Keith Wilkes, and their teammates—continued to play at near their highest level of competency and outscored Notre Dame 82–63 to set the new record for consecutive victories. Afterward, for one of the very few times in my coaching career, I allowed reporters into the locker room to interview the players because it was such a special occasion.

So when the streak finally ended a year later in 1974, it was fine with me. Any loss stings, but our loss in the 89th game stung no more than any other, which is to say, a lot, but not because it ended the streak.

UNEXPECTED CONSEQUENCES?

Something seldom mentioned, however, is the effect the winning streak had on the remainder of our 1974 season. Is it possible that it adversely affected what followed? Could it perhaps, I say *perhaps*, have cost us a national championship?

The accumulated stress on the players over nearly two and a half seasons—Bill Walton, Keith Wilkes, Tommy Curtis, Greg Lee, David Meyers, and the others—was impossible to measure, but presumably extreme. A squad that had won 73 games in a row (after their predecessors had won the initial 15 consecutive games) and two straight national championships was suddenly released from the pressure cooker of having to be "perfect" every single game. What happened after that is hard to measure.

In the remaining games of that 1974 season after the streak was broken by Notre Dame, we lost back-to-back games to Oregon State and Oregon, nearly lost to Stanford, and then had the overtime disappointments of the Final Four with Dayton and North Carolina State. Something seemed to have happened after the streak was broken by Notre Dame in the 88th game.

Talent is God-given; be humble.

Fame is man-given; be thankful.

Conceit is self-given; be careful.

THE FINAL BUZZER AT UCLA

I didn't know I was going to retire until the moment I retired. Lots of rumors were going around, and some people claimed to know it was coming, but how could they if I didn't? When it happened, Nell was surprised, UCLA was surprised, and I was surprised. J. D. Morgan, our athletic director, was not surprised—he was flabbergasted.

At the beginning of the 1974–75 season, my last, the Bruins had a clean slate for the first time in many years; that is, our 88-game winning streak, the run of seven straight NCAA championships, and 38 consecutive victories in tournament play had all ended the previous season. Furthermore, Bill Walton, Keith Wilkes, Greg Lee, and Tommy Curtis—great players—were gone. The squad had only one returning starter, David Meyers, and he was surrounded by a team most people viewed as considerably less capable than their immediate and famous predecessors.

A FINAL RUN

For only the third time in my entire coaching career, I appointed a captain for the entire season rather than from game to game. (I had learned at South Bend Central that when teams elect their own captain, it generally becomes a popularity contest. Popularity, in my opinion, is not one of the essentials of leadership.)

David Meyers was not only an All-American athlete, but a captain who led by example more than by words, a fierce competitor whose teammates were kind people helped by his aggressive example. Meyers's work ethic had one gear: high speed. David reminded me of my own style when I was at Purdue; he dove after loose balls, fought for everything, and played with a zeal that affected the whole team. The results were gratifying.

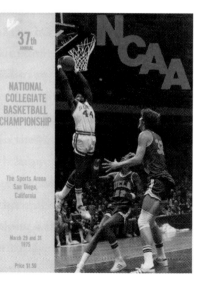
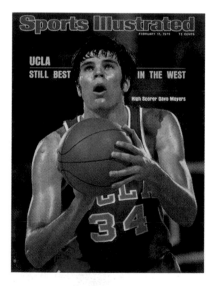

The end was near. I sat alone in the San Diego Sports Arena.

To the surprise of many, Marques Johnson, Richard Washington, Pete Trgovich, Andre McCarter, Ralph Drollinger, and David Meyers of the UCLA Bruins returned to the Final Four again—our twelfth trip in fourteen years. It was held at San Diego's Sports Arena where we faced Louisville in the semifinals, in what became a memorable game. At the end of regulation play, the score was 65–65.

There is no such thing as a perfect game, but this one may have come very close. It's a shame we had to continue; both teams had performed so well and played so hard under such great pressure.

I got so riled up near the end of the Louisville semifinal that one of the officials came over to make sure I didn't run out onto the court. He calmly said, "John, the referee can hear you fine from right here."

David and his teammates went on to outscore Louisville 75–74 in
overtime to advance to the championship game. At the final buzzer, the
spectators were in near-hysteria and reminded me of the pandemonium
in 1928 when Charlie Secrist's desperation shot defeated the Martinsville Artesians in the final seconds of the Indiana state championship.

I slowly made my way through the mob onto the court and shook
hands with Louisville's coach, Denny Crum, my former assistant and
good friend. I told him what a fine game his team had played, and he
congratulated me and the Bruins. Then I turned and began working my
way to the pressroom for the postgame interview.

Suddenly I felt almost ill, but I wasn't sick. I just couldn't bring myself to talk to reporters about the game. I don't know exactly why, but something in my head just said, "It's over." I slowly veered off to the Bruins' locker room, where the players were in a joyous mood following their wonderful performance. As they saw me enter,

the noise got even louder, perhaps because they thought I'd come to join in the excitement, but that's not why I was there.

SAYING GOOD-BYE

Somebody pulled up a chair for me to stand on, and everyone gathered around as I waited for them to quiet down. I congratulated the young men on their performance and the hard work they had done throughout the entire season, told them the game was almost perfect, and that Louisville was a worthy opponent who gave the victory meaning.

Then I told them why I was there: "You've given me as much pleasure as any team I've ever coached, and never caused a single problem on

or off the court. I want to thank you for that. It means so much to me, because you are the last team I will ever coach. I'm bowing out."

Ducky Drake, who for almost thirty years had been our trainer and my friend, almost fainted. The boys were stunned and silent. I got down off the chair and forced myself to go into the pressroom.

I began the question-and-answer session with my short announcement: "I'm asking Athletic Director J. D. Morgan to relieve me of my duties as head coach of UCLA at the conclusion of this tournament."

My only regret is that my statement took attention off the game and shifted it onto my decision. The game—near-perfect basketball by both teams—deserved all the attention; reporters, however, wanted to know about my announcement. But there really wasn't more to tell them.

Later that evening in my hotel room, J. D. Morgan spent half the night trying to talk me out of retiring. Nell, however, didn't try to talk me out of it.

Forty-eight hours later, David Meyers and his teammates won UCLA's tenth NCAA basketball championship by defeating Kentucky 92–85.

NO REAL ANSWER

I still can only guess at why I chose to retire when I did. If you'd asked me before the Louisville game what my plans were, I'd have said honestly, "I'm coaching one more year for sure, maybe two, and then I'll retire." But at the end of that semifinal game against Denny's team—a

What is success? For many it's trophies or blue ribbons. That's why this publicity shot was taken—to show how successful our teams had been. But I don't measure it like that. The highest success is in your effort—giving it your personal best.

beautifully played game as any I'd seen—something happened inside and I just didn't want to go on with it anymore.

Perhaps it was Nell's health, which had increasingly concerned me. I was very good when it came to not worrying about those things that

I could not control—Dad had taught me that. But Nell's health was different. I just couldn't stop worrying about it. How much it got to me I can't say, but it may have been why my energy, vitality, and spirits had gone down through the year. I wasn't really the same person anymore.

Even though I had a little heart problem in 1973, I felt great soon afterward. Something else must have been going on inside me. I really can't give you a better explanation.

But for me, coaching was over.

THE GREAT LOSS AND LOVE

Nell suffered under the stress and strain of being married to a coach. The profession brings with it automatic criticism, and dear Nellie, my biggest fan, couldn't stand hearing me criticized; it caused her such pain.

When you lose, you're criticized for losing. When you win, after a while you're criticized for not winning by enough. (Immediately following the final game of my career, UCLA's victory over Kentucky for a tenth national championship, a fan shook my hand and yelled, "Way to go, Coach! You let us down last year, but you came through this time." I had "let him down" by not winning another national championship.) The criticism and impossibly high expectations really hurt Nell inside, and she agonized through each basketball season—even the winning streaks— in a way I didn't.

So retirement was just fine for both of us. I conducted coaching clinics, did some play-by-play broadcasting, and Nell and I traveled and enjoyed life together. We were a couple of lucky people who loved being with each other more than anything. I recognized it the day I felt that spark back in high school, and I have told friends my greatest personal accomplishment was the day Nell Riley said, "I do."

THE BEGINNING OF THE END

We enjoyed our days together very much, but Nell's health continued to worsen in the next few years. In 1984, she entered the hospital for surgery that was complicated by emphysema and heart trouble. Shortly

afterward she went into a coma, and doctors told me she'd never come out of it.

I spent all of my days at her bedside and slept many nights on a small cot next to her in the hospital room. The specialists held out little hope, but they said it wouldn't hurt to talk to her even though she couldn't hear me.

So I held Nell's hand while I recalled our life together—the malteds at Shireman's Ice Cream Parlor and silent movies at the Grace Theatre; avoiding Coach Curtis on dates during basketball season; the $200 Cliff Schnaiter gave us to get married and then being apart our first week of marriage so I could earn money at Piggy Lambert's basketball camp; the excitement of moving to Dayton, Kentucky, and setting up house together; and the arrival of Nancy Ann, our beautiful, sweet little daughter.

I reminded Nell how proud she was—me, too—when our son, Jimmy, was born a few years later. And I talked about our friends in Centerton, Martinsville, Dayton, West Lafayette, South Bend, Terre Haute, and Los Angeles. I recalled our little ritual before each basketball game—she'd give me the thumbs-up sign and I'd give her the OK sign. I said the Good Lord was watching over her and that I was praying she would get better. I told Nell how much I loved her.

But there was never the slightest response from her—nothing. So I just kept talking.

One afternoon after weeks and weeks of sharing my memories, I stopped for a moment and took a little break. As I sat there in the sterile room staring out the window and holding Nell's hand, there was a tiny little squeeze—almost imperceptible. I couldn't believe it, and I thought it was my imagination. But I started talking again, and every now and then my hand would get another little squeeze from her. It wasn't my imagination. Nell was slowly coming out of the coma. It had lasted for ninety days.

My joy was indescribable—the girl I loved, my sweetheart of sixty years—had come back to me. It may have been some kind of miracle, I don't know. Our family arrived, and a few days later Nell was home.

Although her condition wasn't good, Nell's laughter and Irish sense of humor were intact and our house, dark and cold for months, was now filling up with love. I was looking forward to the years ahead.

But on Christmas Eve she got terribly sick again, and I rushed her to the hospital. Nell was a good little fighter and fought long and hard, but this time it was different. On the first day of spring—Thursday, March 21, 1985—the Good Lord released my little sweetheart from her pain.

MY GREAT SORROW

If you dropped a small pebble into the deepest part of the ocean on the darkest night of the year—that was me without Nell. Her death brought grief down on me in a terrible way. I was desolate, unable to function day after day, week after week; I was alone, immobilized by what seemed unendurable.

Family and friends, coaches and former players tried to bring comfort, but it was useless. I'm ashamed to say that I even questioned my faith. I became almost a recluse and didn't care to do anything or see anyone. This went on for months; it seemed like years. I was just unable to come out of it, inconsolable without Nell.

Later I was told by those closest to me that they feared for my life. I don't know, they may have been right.

A DOOR CLOSES, ANOTHER OPENS

Although I didn't recognize it at the time, that same year, 1985—the one that brought such sorrow—also brought my survival, the birth of Nell's and my first great-grandchild, Cori. Initially, I hardly took notice of the blessing, because I was too deep in grief. But she is the reason I began recovering.

The Good Lord first took Nell, but then sent the love of Cori and great-grandchild after great-grandchild until their love and the love of all our grandchildren was everywhere around me like a field full of flowers. And then a very special gift was sent, a great-grandchild named Cameron, most severely handicapped in every way except his unlimited capacity to give love and create it in others. Slowly I began getting back my old self as I saw in their smiles, laughter, and love Nell's own smile, laughter, and love. She is them and they are her.

All of this was, and is, amazing and wonderful.

A GREAT DAY IS COMING

Certainly the old must make way for the new, however painful that may be. Nell was taken, but my life was renewed when I recognized and accepted the love of Cori and her little brothers, sisters, and cousins. Everywhere I look, then and now, I see Nell. Everywhere I look, I see the Good Lord's plan.

The deep sense of loss I feel without my sweetheart has never gone away, not for one single day. But the spirit of love I've regained is

The sorrow started to leave when Cori arrived.

stronger than ever, and it gets stronger each day. I was never preoccupied with dying. But perhaps like most people, I feared it. Losing Nell has cured me of any fear of death because I believe that when I'm called, when the Good Lord beckons according to his plan, I will go to heaven and be with her. Knowing this gives me peace.

EACH DAY OF THE JOURNEY IS PRECIOUS. WE MUST STRIVE TO MAKE IT A MASTERPIECE.

Mind you, I'm in no hurry to leave, but I have no fear of leaving. When the time comes, it will be a very good day—Nell and I will be together again. In the meantime, each day of the journey is precious, yours and mine—we must strive to make it a masterpiece. Each day, once gone, is gone forever.

My father's words and deeds—his wisdom—taught me that and more. He gave me a direction I continue to try to live up to. His advice was good and his example even better. My mentors, Earl Warriner, Glenn Curtis, and Ward "Piggy" Lambert shared their knowledge and wisdom as all great teachers do. Their interest in students went beyond the basketball court or even the classroom. They wanted to help us have good lives.

I've tried to live up to my mentors' examples in teaching those young people who've made my life so rich along the way. My goal has always been to help them become not only better basketball players or English students, but better people. That's the most important thing a coach or teacher can do, and I have given it my personal best.

And as I hope you find in your own life, none of it amounts to a hill of beans without the love of family and friends. I'm a very fortunate man who has much to be thankful for. *Love* is the most important word in the English language, and my journey has been filled with so much love. I pray that yours is too—that your own journey is full of love.

And that along the way you never cease trying to be the best *you* can be— that you always strive for your personal best.

That is success. And don't let anybody tell you otherwise.

*Cam is a special child
whose gift is love.*

These players I coached—all of them—are like members of my extended family. And my love for them is strong. When UCLA gave the great honor of renaming the court at Pauley Pavillion the Nell and John Wooden Court, many, many of those players were there. Those who couldn't attend were there in my heart. Somewhere Nell was smiling.

CREDITS

Sports Illustrated: p. x; p. 102 (©Neil Leifer); p. 120 (©Hy Peskin); p. 128 (©Rick Clarkson); p. 129 (©Neil Leifer); p. 143; p. 149 (©Neil Leifer, ©Rick Clarkson, ©James Drake); p. 162 (©James Drake); p. 171(©Sheedy & Long, ©Rick Clarkson, ©Carl Iwasaki); p. 188 (©Neil Leifer); pp. 206–207 (©John W. McDonough)

AP Wide World Photos: p. 83; p. 90; p. 91; p. 153; p. 158; p. 167; p. 183; p. 184; p. 190; p. 192

ASUCLA: p. 89; p. 94; p. 97; p. 99; p. 100; p. 105; p. 109; p. 121; p. 122; p. 126; p. 130; p. 132; p. 137; p. 139; p. 144; p. 151; p. 152; p. 155; p. 160; p. 164; p. 165; p.166; p. 172; p. 173; p. 175; p. 176; p. 189; p. 191; p 195; p. 198; p. 200

Tom Casalini: p. iii

Bob Poppino: p. 20

Purdue Sports Information Office/Special Collection Library: p.38; 39; 42; 43; 44; 46; 48; 53

Indiana State University Archives—Athletic Photograph Collection: p. 71; pp. 72–73; p. 78; p. 81

Terre Haute Star: p. 82

South Bend Tribune: p. 62; p. 64; p. 65

The Queens Borough Public Library, Long Island Division, *New York-Herald Tribune* Collection: p. 148

NCAA: p. 133 (©Rick Clarkson); pp. 134–135 (©Rick Clarkson); p. 148; p. 163; p.171; p. 188 (©Rick Clarkson); p. 193 (©Rick Clarkson)

Roy Stark: p. 80

Los Angeles Times: p. 203 (©Anacleto Rapping)

All other images courtesy of John Wooden